Food photography by Howard Shooter

Published by Stonewash DD&AG Ltd
55 Farringdon Road, London EC1M 3JB, United Kingdom

ISBN 978-0-9567224-0-9

RUSSIA
ON A PLATE

KARINA BALDRY

FOR REGULAR UPDATES PLEASE VISIT THE SITE
RUSSIAONAPLATE.COM

Dedicated to my family.

I am a co-founder of the charity Chance for Life.

The idea behind Chance for Life is to provide
additional assistance to several charitable
organisations supporting orphanages in Russia.

Some of the proceeds from the sale of this
book will be donated to this charity.

For more information please go to www.chanceforlife.co.uk.

"Everything I do, I do on the principle of Russian borscht. You can throw everything into it beets, carrots, cabbage, onions, everything you want. What's important is the result, the taste of the borscht."

Yevgeny Yevtushenko, Russian poet

"It was the best of times, it was the worst of times... it was the spring of hope, it was the winter of despair, we had everything before us, we had nothing before us, we were all going direct to Heaven, we were all going direct the other way..."

Charles Dickens 'A Tale of Two Cities'

PREFACE

I grew up in a society where everything Western seemed to be covered in chocolate.

Of course, I later realised that this perception was nothing but a romantic fairytale. A fascination bordering on an obsession. Anything west of the Polish border invoked inexplicable curiosity and gave out the impression of abundance, luxury and of a carefree lifestyle. Blue jeans. Chewing gum. The Beatles...!

Only once the curtain had parted, when I too could not only visit but actually (who'd have believed it) live in the West, did I appreciate the more nuanced truth. And, as we grow up and become more aware of the everyday problems of our present, we also continue to appreciate some of what we had, all those years ago.

Yes, I have travelled a long way from the Soviet collective apartments of my childhood. But, like anyone who leaves their Motherland, one long gone place always exerts an everlasting draw – the kitchen of our childhood.

This book is my love letter to the recipes that not only fed me and nourished me but provided me with pure, genuine happiness because we were happy. Truly.

Whether in our tiny state apartment, in a block erected in a muddy field outside Moscow or the hot summers spent at my grandmother's, in the small town of Pyatigorsk in the Caucasus, I remember small kitchens filled with laughter and gorgeous smells.

Caviar and vodka have their place. Today, caviar is so exorbitantly expensive as to be nothing but a luxurious treat. But vodka, I will happily admit, does have its purpose.

What I want you, the reader and adventurous cook, to appreciate, is two things about Soviet-era food. Firstly, it's essentially what it is fashionably termed 'fusion food'. Such a huge landmass - 22.4 million square kilometres! - taking in 15 republics and more than 100 ethnic groups, from the edge of the Baltic Sea to the vast steppes of Siberia to the basking hot deserts of Central Asia, stretching halfway around the world - couldn't help but give rise to an amazingly diverse cuisine.

Secondly, Russian food is healthy food. Our parents and grandparents had to be physically active workers. Our staples of kasha – savoury or sweet cooked cereals made from buckwheat, semolina, pearl barley or rice – and soups like schi and borscht were cheap, tasty, high in fibre, low in fat and, most importantly, in the days when we didn't have that much choice, lasted days in the fridge (where they actually got better).

It strikes me that my childhood diet might not be a bad way for westerners to stay fitter and healthier for longer. There are, of course, many richer, spicier and more indulgent recipes in these pages, too. I have tried to give them a modern twist, to incorporate Western ingredients and to take account of today's lifestyle limitations. We don't all have a spare babushka we can leave to stir the pot for a few hours...

Each chapter marks out recipes that come from a different stage of my journey, from the communal apartments of 60's Moscow, to the laid-back summers in the northern Caucasus, to the exciting (and sometimes unsettling) changes brought about by perestroika. You may find much in them that seems exotic or strange. But optimism never fails me – a quality which was acquired through the years living under communism – and I am hopeful that you are open-minded and that your heart (and stomach) are ready to embrace our little Russian specialities.

Na Zdorovje!

01

LIVING

GOOD BAD OLD TIMES

Some memories will always remain vivid by their uniqueness. I would like to take you back several decades; to a Soviet apartment where my grandparents and parents are cooking, dancing around the kitchen stove along with their other housemates in conditions that can be politely described as 'bizarre'.

In the early years of communism, the Party introduced a new concept: communal flats. This meant that, instead of one family enjoying the apartment, four or five families found themselves living alongside each other sharing a common kitchen and bathroom.

The choice was simple. You either had to have a great sense of humour or incredible tolerance of your neighbours, to stay sane. Most of your fellow inhabitants were definitely not going to be your soul mates – just getting along was the name of the game. Queues for the bathroom were a usual morning routine.

In the kitchen, the principle of 'first come, first served' was maintained. Come late and you were running the risk of being left without breakfast. Most people kept their fridges and some kitchen utensils in their personal rooms which made their living space even more cluttered. There was a reason for this; often cheeky neighbours would steal food or worse, you could find an unpleasant surprise in your saucepan if one of them had a bone to pick with you!

So you can imagine my utter joy, when at the age of five, my family moved into our own 3-room apartment, with our own bathroom, a kitchen and, most importantly, NO neighbours to fight with. Luxury.

Obviously, sacrifices had to be made. We had to move out from the heart of

Moscow to the outskirts. I'll never forget; we had been walking for about 40 minutes through an extremely rural and uninhabited countryside. Orchards, berry bushes, deserted wooden huts and desolate village wells but no bus and not a living soul in sight. Then, in the middle of a muddy field, I spotted in the distance six white high-rise buildings. It was a triumph!

I remember running around the place overwhelmed, whereas my parents had their doubts. My mother was a ballerina who had trained at the Bolshoi and my father was a saxophonist. They probably felt that being in the middle of nowhere kept them from the bustling, creative energy of the city. It didn't help that the three rooms covered just 55 square metres, including the kitchen and the bathroom. But at least our new home was just ours. Nowadays, North West Moscow is a prestigious area, heavily developed with a rich infrastructure. Times do change.

Even such cramped conditions could not stop Russians from cooking and entertaining. How they managed to do that remains a mystery even to me – I put it down to our cheerful Russian stoicism in the face of any obstacle. In a standard 5 square metre Russian kitchen, one pot meals such as stews, kashas and soups were the most efficient use of space. And they tasted good, too.

Although soup is a well-loved dish in the West, through my personal experience, I have come to the conclusion that kasha needs a lot of working on before it's appealing. I personally love buckwheat; even the aroma from the pan when it's bubbling away. The form of buckwheat available in the UK is different to that available in Russia – English buckwheat is not roasted and it doesn't have that characteristic brown colour and nutty taste that immediately takes me back to my childhood.

It's completely under-rated, too; the nutritious values of buckwheat are very high.

Low calories and a great source of iron make it a perfect addition to a GI diet. However, I realise that not everyone feels the same way as I do. Once, I was excited to serve buckwheat to my English husband just as it comes: a whole plate with just a knob of butter to taste. The result was quite a surprise – he asked me for the ketchup. Mmmm.

I learnt my lesson. Now the challenge for me was to find new ways to use our treasured kashas in a more appealing way whilst still keeping their authenticity. Here they are.

NOT VERY TRADITIONAL BORSCHT

NE OCHEN TRADITZIONNY BORSCHT

It's hard to think of anything more Russian than Borscht; it used to be a staple in a Russian kitchen. This particular recipe is my version and differs from the one you find in a traditional Russian cookbook but is my personal favourite. It has been developed through trial and error and it's as tasty as the conventional one but takes half the time.

Hands on time: 35-40 minutes   **Serves:** 5-6 people

Ingredients:

2 ltrs vegetable stock or a good quality vegetable stock cube

2 small raw beetroots, coarsely grated

1 medium onion, chopped

1 big carrot, coarsely grated

2 garlic cloves, sliced

3 tbsp tomato ketchup

½ tsp hot chili spice blend (optional, see the comment on page 58)

2 tbsp tomato sauce (recipe on page 79)

3-4 tbsp vegetable oil

170g white cabbage, shredded

3 medium potatoes, cubed

3 tbsp fresh chopped mixed herbs (such as dill, flat leaf parsley, coriander)

Salt and pepper for seasoning

Heat the oil in a large frying pan. Sauté the beetroot, carrots, onion and garlic for about 7-10 minutes over a gentle heat, stirring regularly. Season well with salt and pepper. Don't put too much salt in at this stage as vegetable stock can be quite salty - you can always adjust the seasoning later. Add the ketchup, tomato sauce and chili paste (if you're using it). Continue cooking on a low heat for a further 5 minutes and then set aside. Meanwhile, prepare the vegetable stock and bring it to the boil. Put the cooked vegetable mixture into the stock, stir well, reduce the heat and let it simmer for about 5 minutes. Then add the shredded cabbage. After 5-7 minutes, add the cubed potatoes. Taste and adjust the seasoning accordingly. Cook partially covered for a further 15 minutes on a medium heat or until the potatoes are tender. Toss in the fresh herbs a couple of minutes before the end. I always think it's better to eat Borscht the next day when all the flavours are incorporated. So plan it in advance! I like to serve Borscht with a dollop of sour cream, a slice of Russian rye bread or any type of rye bread topped with parsley butter (see the recipe on page 20). You can also sprinkle fresh parsley on top for additional flavour and colour. Be generous with herbs!

PARSLEY BUTTER

It is fantastic to spread this butter on Russian Borodinsky Bread or any other type of rye bread you can find and have it with Borscht. This butter is quite versatile. Here are a couple of suggestions: mix it in mashed potatoes or use it to top baked fish such as sea bass. (See stockists for bread on page 124).

Ingredients:

100g of butter, softened not melted
3 tbsp of fresh parsley, chopped
Salt and freshly ground black pepper
1 tsp of paprika
1 crushed garlic clove

Method:

Take 100g out of the fridge and keep it at room temperature for at least an hour. Mash the softened butter slightly with a fork and then stir in chopped parsley, salt and freshly ground black pepper and paprika to taste. Cool the butter in the fridge for 10 minutes otherwise it will be too soft to shape it. After cooling, roll the butter in wet greaseproof paper into the shape of a log and chill until firm. Re-wrap in cling film and twist each end to seal. The butter will keep in the fridge for 5 days or in the freezer for up to 3 months.

HOMEY SOUP WITH BABY MEATBALLS

DOMASHNY SUP S MINI FRIKADELKAMI

There is something really comforting in going to the fridge and finding a pot of soup that you can snack on. And this soup is great for this occasion. If you feel peckish a bowl of soup is a much healthier option than a packet of crisps! It keeps well in the fridge for up to three days.

Hands on time: 30 minutes   **Serves:** 4-6 people

Ingredients for the meatballs:

200g lean minced beef
1 shallot or half a small onion, finely chopped
¼ sweet pepper (any color), finely grated
½ tsp granulated garlic or one small crushed garlic
½ tsp paprika
1 tbsp vegetable oil
2 tbsp cold water
1 tbsp chopped fresh herbs (dill, parsley)
Salt and pepper

Ingredients for the stock:

1½ ltrs beef stock (you can use good quality beef stock cubes)
1 medium carrot, cubed
½ parsnip, cubed,
½ sweet pepper (any color), cubed
3 medium potatoes (about 350g), cubed
2 bay leaves
5-7 black peppercorns

Prepare the mince. Grate a quarter of the sweet pepper by pressing its skinless side to the fine grater. Discard the skin. I find it adds additional flavour to the mince and makes it more moist. Mix all the ingredients for the meatballs together. Set aside.

Make 1½ litres of beef stock in a saucepan and bring it to the boil. Put the vegetables, except the potatoes, for the stock in the saucepan. Lower the heat to medium and simmer for about 5-7 minutes. Start forming meatballs about the size of a cherry (this amount will make 35-40 meatballs) and put them straight into the boiling stock. Simmer for about 7 minutes. Add cubed potatoes, a couple of bay leaves and black peppercorns and simmer for another 10-12 minutes or until potatoes are tender but not falling apart. Adjust seasonings. Remove bay leaves from the saucepan before serving. Sprinkle with chopped fresh herbs.

The size of the meatballs doesn't really matter. I personally prefer them rather small. But each to his own!

CHILLED CUCUMBER SOUP WITH SMOKED SALMON

KHOLODNY SUP IZ OGURTSOV S KOPCHJONIM LOSOSEM

It is a Dacha's summer favourite dish – easy, refreshing and zingy but equally, it can be fit for elegant dining, as a starter.

Hands on time: 15 minutes, plus chilling time   **Serves:** 6 people

Ingredients:

400g cucumber
200g natural yoghurt
1 tsp lemon juice
2 tbsp chopped dill
Splash of Tabasco sauce
200g smoked salmon

Slice the cucumber and place it into a bowl. Season with salt and pepper and leave it to stand for about 10 minutes at room temperature. Blend the cucumber with yoghurt, lemon juice and Tabasco. Adjust seasonings. Pour the mixture into a bowl, cover it and put it in the fridge for about 2 hours or until you need it. Chop smoked salmon into small pieces. When you are ready to serve, pour the soup into serving bowls.

If you serve the soup as a starter for smart entertaining I would recommend serving it in espresso cups or clear glasses.

KARINA'S BEETROOT AND APPLE SALAD
SVEKOLNO-JABLOCHNY SALAT

I don't want to imply anything here other than mention the fact that this salad used to bear my name. I was always passionate about beetroot and we used to cook it or roast it most of the time. I wanted to try and use raw beetroot and perk it up with apples and cucumber for freshness and gherkins for sharpness. And what we have here is a mid-season accompaniment for meat or as a part of Russian Zakuski spread. Fulsome and refreshing – a salad for many occasions.

Hands on time: 15 minutes   **Serves:** 6-8 people

Ingredients:

2 small raw beetroots, grated

2 small raw carrots, grated

1 small apple, finely cubed

2.5cm cucumber, cubed

3 small dill pickled cucumbers or gherkins, finely cubed (see stockists on page 124)

1 shallot or half a small onion, finely chopped

2 heaped tbsp of fresh mixed herbs (parsley, coriander, dill)

2 tbsp of mayonnaise or just enough to bind the salad together

Mix all the ingredients together in a big bowl. Season the salad with salt and pepper. Prepare this dish about 3 hours before serving to let the flavours incorporate.

OLD STYLE PATÉ PANCAKE STACK
BLINCHATY PIROG

Using inexpensive ingredients – pancakes and chicken livers – makes these a great choice in times of economic wobbles. Once made, keep them in the fridge for easy snacking, lunches and light suppers. You can eat this versatile dish warm or cold. All you need is a little green salad on the side and a dollop of crème fraîche.

Hands on time: 40 minutes   **Serves:** 6 people

Ingredients for the chicken liver filling:

600g chicken livers
1 onion, chopped
1 medium raw carrot, coarsely grated
1 small raw parsnip, coarsely grated
4 tbsp orange juice
1 tbsp vodka
2-3 tbsp sour cream or 3-4 tbsp of chicken stock or water
2-3 tbsp fresh herbs, such as parsley or dill, finely chopped
Salt and pepper

See page 49 for pancake recipe

Wash, pat dry and trim chicken livers. Heat a couple of tablespoons of vegetable oil in a pan. Pan-fry the livers for about 5 minutes before adding chopped onion, grated carrot, parsnip and a knob of butter. Continue cooking for a further 5-6 minutes. Add 5 tablespoons of orange juice and simmer for about 3 minutes. Season well. Let it cool slightly. Mince in a food processor. Return the mixture to the pan, add vodka, 2-3 tablespoons of sour cream, quickly cook it through for about 1 minute and add chopped herbs. If you do not want to use sour cream, you can just add a bit of chicken stock or water to make the mixture more moist. It should resemble a smooth paté and be easily spreadable. Lay one pancake on a plate and spread some chicken liver mixture on it. Continue layering with pancakes and chicken liver mixture - I use 4-5 pancakes for the given quantity of the pate. When the stack is formed, sprinkle with the rest of the herbs and serve.

ALEXANDER'S PILAF
SASHIN PLOV

This recipe is based on a traditional **Central Asian Pilaf but I first tried it when it was prepared by my relative, Alexander, in Moscow. Since then, I have always called it by his name. It is an ideal crowd pleaser. A fabulous one pot dish to have as a centrepiece in the middle of the table for people to dip into.**

Hands on time: 75 minutes   **Serves:** 6 people

Ingredients:

1kg lamb neck fillet, cut into bite size pieces

A squeeze of lemon

380g long grained rice

300g onion, sliced

300g carrots, coarsely grated

3 medium garlic bulbs, unpeeled and smashed with the side of a broad knife

3-4 tbsp vegetable oil

10 dried barberries (Asian spice)

3 heaped tsp pilaf spice

Generous helping of fresh coriander, chopped

Salt and pepper to taste

If you can't find barberries (see stockists on page 124 for details) you can replace them with dried cranberries or dried sour cherries.

Cut lamb into bite size pieces, season well with salt and pepper and a squeeze of lemon and leave to stand for about 2 hours or you can prepare the meat the night before. Grate carrots and slice the onions. Heat the oil in a big wok type pan until it is very hot. Stir fry the lamb pieces till they are well browned. Add the onion and 5 minutes later, the carrots, garlic and barberries. Stir fry the mixture for another 5-7 minutes. Add the pilaf spice and rice. Stir it well until the rice is well coated in oil. Cook for about 2 minutes. Pour 4 cups of boiling water into the pan. Cook it on a high heat until the water reduces to under the level of the rice. At this point, lower the heat and cook for another 20 minutes without stirring. After 10 minutes make holes all around the rice with a teaspoon or a knife to help the water to evaporate. After another 10 minutes, cover the pan with a lid and let it simmer on a very low heat until the rice is tender. Sprinkle with fresh coriander. Adjust seasoning if necessary.

If you are not very keen on unpeeled garlic then you can use peeled garlic cloves instead. You can buy Pilaf Spice in almost any supermarket but if you'd like to go the extra mile to be more authentic, you will have to visit either an Asian or a Russian shop.

BASIC BUCKWHEAT

Buckwheat does require a bit more time to prepare than quick varieties of couscous. But it is a very healthy grain and once you get used to its taste you will love it, as all Russians do. You can vary it by adding fried onion and bacon, herbs and tomatoes or whatever you fancy!

Ingredients:

250g roasted buckwheat
500ml boiling water
Pinch of salt
1 tsp brown sugar
A knob of butter

Method:

Take out the impurities from the grain by rinsing the buckwheat in cold water. Drain. Put it in a saucepan with the salt, sugar and butter. Pour the boiling water over it. Bring to the boil and cook it uncovered until the water level is under the buckwheat. Then put the lid on the saucepan and simmer for about 15-20 minutes. Check it once in a while to make sure it doesn't get dry. Add some more water if needed. And it's done.

POACHED CHICKEN BREASTS

Here's my recipe for poached chicken breasts. They shouldn't take you any more than 30 minutes to prepare and cook. This recipe is great for the Chicken in Walnut Sauce on page 85.

Ingredients:

4 boneless skinless chicken breasts

750ml chicken stock or enough to cover the chicken

4 tsp dried mixed herbs

2 bay leaves

Method:

Place the chicken breasts in a heavy-bottomed pot. They should fit in a single layer but fit quite snugly. Cover chicken with the chicken stock. Add the herbs and bay leaves.

Bring to the boil and then quickly reduce the heat to low so that the water is barely at a simmer. Partly cover and gently simmer for 10 minutes. Turn off the heat completely and allow the chicken to remain in the hot water for 15-20 minutes, then remove.

MY STIR FRIED POTATOES

KARTOSHECHKA ZHARENAJA

This recipe is one of the essential ones in my everyday family menu. The recipe for the stir fried potatoes was passed down from generation to generation. My Mum used to make them for me and I loved eating fried potatoes straight from a frying pan. They are great just for snacking with some cut up cucumber and radishes or brilliant with a steak. My son refers to them as "Can you please make "your potatoes" for me, Mum?"

Hands on time: 15 minutes   **Serves:** 6 as a side dish, 4 as a snack

Ingredients to make thin pancakes:

6 medium potatoes, sliced into thin chip-size pieces
2-3 tbsp vegetable oil
Knob of butter
Salt and pepper
Handful of fresh herbs (parsley, dill or coriander), chopped

Peel potatoes. Slice them into quite thin chip-size pieces. Heat 2 tablespoons of vegetable oil in a frying pan until quite hot. Lower the heat down to medium. Add potatoes and a knob of butter. Stir fry potatoes on a medium heat for about 10 minutes stirring frequently until they are an even golden colour. If necessary, add a bit more oil. When cooked, season with salt and pepper.

For extra flavour you can sprinkle them with chopped fresh herbs whichever you have to hand – parsley, dill or even coriander for a more Caucasian flavour.

CHICKEN BREASTS STUFFED WITH BUCKWHEAT AND BACON

KURINIJE GRUDKI NACHINJENIJE GRECHKOY I BEKONOM

I would like my favourite grain – buckwheat - to be used in more recipes so I thought, breadcrumbs and couscous work well as a stuffing - why not buckwheat?

Hands on time: 45 minutes + cooking buckwheat   **Serves:** 6 people

Ingredients:

6 chicken breasts, boneless and skinless

100g uncooked buckwheat grains (see stockists on page 124)

20g coriander, finely chopped

5 rashers back bacon, chopped

1 small onion, finely chopped

4 tbsp any fruit chutney of your choice

4 tbsp plain flour for dusting

500ml chicken gravy

2 tbsp vegetable oil for frying

Rinse 100g uncooked buckwheat in a colander under running water. Shake off the excess water. Put it in a saucepan and pour over 200ml of boiling water with a pinch of salt and a pinch of sugar. Bring it to the boil and simmer for about 15-20 minutes. Check half way through the cooking time by making a hole with a knife to see if the water has evaporated and, if necessary, add a little more water. Add a knob of butter towards the end of the cooking time. For this recipe you will need 120g of cooked buckwheat, see the method on page 27.

Pre-heat the oven to 180℃ / gas mark 4. Using a rolling pin, flatten the chicken breasts between two pieces of cling film or in a plastic bag. Season them on both sides with salt and pepper.

Heat the oil in a frying pan and fry the bacon for about 3 minutes and then add the onion and continue sautéing for a further 4 minutes until the onion is soft. Mix the onion and bacon into the cooked buckwheat with the coriander and fruit chutney. Season the mixture with salt and pepper to your taste. Put approximately 1 tablespoon of the mixture into the middle of each chicken breast. Roll them up into the shape of a roulade and secure with cocktail sticks. Dust roulades in flour. Heat the oil in a frying pan and brown them on both sides. Transfer chicken roulades into an ovenproof casserole dish with the lid on. Make enough chicken gravy to cover the roulades. Put them into the oven for about 30 minutes.

BABUSHKA'S POTATO CAKES WITH MUSHROOM SAUCE

BABUSHKINI KARTOPHELNIJE KOTLETKI S GRIBNOY PODLIVKOY

My Russian Grandma Claudia's special. This dish was always in demand when I went to visit. It works its warming magic on long winter evenings…

Hands on time: 45 minutes **Makes:** 8 potato cakes

Ingredients for potato cakes::

700g raw peeled potatoes, cooked and mashed
1 egg yolk
2 tbsp flour, if necessary
3 tbsp finely chopped parsley or dill
Salt and black pepper
Knob of butter
See facing page for mushroom sauce

Boil peeled potatoes until tender. Drain and return to the hob for another minute to get rid of excess moisture. Watch the bottom of the pan to ensure that the potatoes don't burn. Coarsely mash the potatoes, add an egg yolk, a knob of butter, the parsley and season to your taste with salt and pepper. If the mixture is too runny, add a couple of tablespoons of flour.

Form 8 cakes, weighing approximately 70g each (you can make them round or oval), dust them with flour and fry in oil on a medium heat until they are golden and heated through in the middle. Put them aside and keep warm.

To serve, put a mixed salad on a plate, place a potato cake on top and pour the hot mushroom sauce over it (see facing page).

This dish can be a substantial starter and also a great vegetarian supper dish. A simple green salad is an ideal base for the potato cakes. The mushroom sauce can also be served as a perfect accompaniment for a steak. You can buy mushroom stock cubes in polish stores or the polish section in most supermarkets – in Polish it is called "Bulion grzybowy" (see stockists on page 124).

MUSHROOM SAUCE

Ingredients:

250g chestnut mushrooms, sliced

30g dried porcini or any other forest mushrooms, soaked and chopped

1 onion, finely chopped

2 tbsp fresh parsley, finely chopped

½ tsp paprika

4 tbsp flour

2 tbsp butter

700ml reserved water from soaked mushrooms

Salt and pepper

Vegetable oil and butter for sautéing

Method:

Rinse the dried mushrooms and soak them in 500ml of cold water overnight. Clean the chestnut mushrooms with a cloth or brush (I prefer not to wash them) and then slice them. Drain the soaked mushrooms and reserve the liquid and then chop them quite fine. Start by dry frying the chestnut mushrooms for about 5-7 minutes until all the juices are evaporated. Add 2 tablespoons of vegetable oil. Put chopped soaked mushrooms into the pan as well as 2 tablespoons of butter. Stir fry for 4-5 min. Add onion and fry for about 5-7 minutes more or until the onion and mushrooms are soft. Set aside. In a separate pan melt 2 tablespoons of butter and mix with 4 tablespoons of plain flour. Make the reserved water from the mushroom up to 700ml with vegetable or mushroom stock from a cube. Gradually start pouring in the stock and continue cooking until the sauce thickens. Stir constantly to avoid lumps. Mix prepared mushrooms into the butter sauce and heat through. Adjust seasoning.

CRUNCHY TWIGS
KHVOROST

These scrumptious "twigs" are fantastic to have on the side, in a big bowl, to munch on as I used to do when I was a child. Children absolutely love them. Beware though they are quite moreish! You can also serve them with ice cream for an after dinner dessert.

Hands on time: 20 minutes   **Serves:** 15 people

Ingredients:

100g flour
1 small egg
1 tsp icing sugar
1 tsp sour cream
1 tsp vodka or brandy
Pinch salt
Icing sugar for dusting

Sieve the flour and the icing sugar in a bowl. Mix in a slightly beaten egg. Still working the egg into the flour, add the sour cream and vodka or brandy. The dough should be quite stiff. If necessary add some more flour. Knead it slightly for a minute or two, form into a ball, cover it with a damp kitchen towel and let it rest for about 15 minutes at room temperature.

Roll out the dough very thinly on a floured surface. Cut into strips - about 2-3cm wide and 8-10cm long. Make a cut in the middle and pull one end of the strip through the cut. Lay them down on a floured surface ready to deep fry. Heat the oil in a pan for deep frying until hot. Depending on the size of the pan put two or three strips at a time into the hot oil. Let them go golden brown, turn once – it will take about 25 seconds. Lift them out with a barbecue skewer or a wooden chopstick and pile them up on a plate covered with kitchen paper. Dust the twigs with icing sugar.

RUSSIAN SNOW APPLE DESSERT

SNEZHNIY JABLOCHNY DESERT

Light and fluffy like the first snow... it is a very pretty looking, elegant and healthy dessert to round off a meal. To show off this dessert in all its beauty, serve it in stylish clear glasses or bowls. It doesn't keep long so make it and serve it up on the day.

Hands on time: 20 minutes   **Serves:** 8 people

Ingredients:

500g apples, peeled, cored and cubed
70g caster sugar
Pinch of nutmeg
Pinch of mixed spice
2 tbsp lemon juice
2 eggs, separated
3 tbsp vodka

Put the apples in a saucepan with the sugar, spices, lemon juice and 2 tablespoons of water. Bring to the boil, cover and simmer gently for about 10 minutes until soft.

Cool slightly and then beat the egg yolks and vodka into the cooled apples and leave to cool completely. You can prepare the dessert up to this stage the day before it is required and keep it in the fridge. On the day whisk the egg whites until stiff and fold them gently into apple mixture. Cover and chill until needed. Before serving divide the apple mixture between clear serving bowls.

Choose your favourite apples; for this recipe I prefer Bramleys.

КРАБ
НАТУРАЛЬНЫЙ
КАМЧАТСКИЙ

БЕЗ КОНСЕРВАНТОВ И КРАСИТЕЛЕЙ !

добыто
и расфасовано
НА КАМЧАТКЕ

ИКРА
ЛОСОСЕВАЯ ЗЕРНИСТАЯ

Печень
ТРЕСКИ
НАТУРАЛЬНАЯ

Масса нетто 230г

VENTSPILS

ZKK

ANNO 1953

Fortunately (or unfortunately), my generation witnessed the transition from socialism to something which I could not even give any proper name. I had known the good times, when food was, at least, accessible and I knew the bad times. There were times when you had to really search for food and then be very inventive, to cook with what you were lucky enough to get. On those days, your dinner was merely bread and spaghetti. Just to get butter to go with it, we had to stand in queues for hours.

Obviously, the availability of certain food items largely influenced the spread on the table. Nevertheless, even in times of hardship, Russian hostesses were saving tins of canned crab for Julienne or canned peas to make Olivier Salad for special occasions, such as a birthday party or a New Year gathering.

Shopping was an involved and complicated process; quite a challenging experience in itself. The average person had to go to the state shops and stand in queues. These were a peculiar phenomenon. Whilst in the shop, you could hear the latest gossip, make friends or even have a quarrel. The whole process of buying was illogical and time-consuming. There were three stages on the way to obtaining food; food counter, cash till and food counter again.

Ready? OK. First of all, you chose the items you wanted from each of the food counters. The sales assistants put them aside whilst you memorised all the prices – the challenge was not to forget them on the way to the cash till. Then you went back to the counter with the paid receipt and finally got hold of your long-awaited goods. God forbid you forgot something or you would have to do the same circle again. By Western standards, some of the food was not even worth queuing for but it was the only available option.

Meat was mostly bones with a little bit of trimming, gamely clinging on for dear life.

Not an attractive sight. The packaging for the food left much to be desired, too - a very rough brown paper that was hardly even foldable!

Ironically, a queue in the shop meant that it could be your lucky day; there was food there. No queue – no food, simple as that. Being a working parent was hard because if anything worth buying appeared in the shops at all, it was usually gone by early afternoon. It was swept away by babushkas (old ladies) who had nothing to do but shop. Picking off the best deals became their profession. It was helpful to have at least one babushka in the household. Many working mums traded their lunch breaks for raiding the shelves in the hope of getting something, anything.

Diplomats and those who worked for foreign companies were proud owners of 'hard currency' and had access to so-called hard currency shops – or 'Beryozka', meaning a birch tree - a symbol of Russia, which was a mockery in itself. (Note from the writer: the official and only currency allowed to circulate in Russia in those days was rubles. Any other currency - dollars, pounds etc., was referred to as 'hard currency'). In those days, these shops were a consumer's paradise. So as not to upset the hard working locals, there were thick shutters and no signs on the windows. Yet most of us knew what was hidden behind them.

Our communist leaders, taking care of their own well-being, had the privilege of buying food in 'specialised shops' which were stocked to the rafters and sold food at unjustifiably low prices.

If you had more money than the average but did not have hard currency, you went to a 'Rynok' - something similar to today's farmers' market. Rynoks were a picturesque sight, full of the lovely smells of fresh herbs and pickles. The farmers came from different parts of Russia and the other Soviet Republics. The market was a vivid showcase of the cosmopolitan nature of our vast country, representing many nations living (and selling) peacefully alongside each other. If there was any tension, it was, at least, well-disguised.

The range of produce on display was very diverse; an abundance of fish products – hot and cold smoked sturgeon, salmon and caviar; home made cheeses and a rich array of vegetables and fruit stacked in the shape of pyramids. The most impressive stalls were of farmers from the Caucasus and Central Asia, with displays so colourful and varied, they represented the full spectrum of our multicultural country. After half an hour walking around the market, your feet might be aching but your mouth was watering. Luckily, we were allowed to try the produce. I remember my family could only afford to go to the markets on special occasions. It had to be a real treat because the prices were biting.

The delights of home grown produce were offered only to the proud owners of a small patch of land outside Moscow, called a 'dacha'. The land was cherished, cultivated and effectively used to the last centimetre. People considered the trip to their dacha as a chore. However, they religiously went to their country retreat every weekend in order to dig, plant, weed and finally pick whatever had been grown in the appropriate season. But the work didn't stop after that; the abundance of fruit and vegetables had to be preserved for a long winter. Cucumbers, sweet peppers and tomatoes were marinated or pickled, cabbage was salted, fruits and berries were transformed into jams and 'kompots', a fruit drink containing the real fruit.

We can envy them now – they were eating 'organic'!

A tiny window into the outside world was opened for some of us in 1980 the year of the Olympic Games in Moscow. For the first time, we realised that outside our country, there was much more than the basic food and unattractive packaging that we took for granted. After the Games, a surplus of the food, supplied mainly by Finland, was piled into the state shops for a very brief period of time which provoked a mini revolution – we saw unbelievable things such as vacuum-packed salami slices, individual jars of jams and tiny cartons of juice with a straw! It sounds funny now but at that time it was amazing. Then, as quickly as it had been opened, that window was shut.

Those days are long gone and we can only look back at it as part of our fascinating history. Fortunately, that spirit of togetherness and sharing what you do have is still a key part of Russian life.

EXPERIMENTAL RUSSIAN FISH CAKES

EKSPERIMENTALNIJE RIBNIJE KOTLETKI

Fish cakes with a difference. I put some of my favorite ingredients together into fish cakes as an experiment and it worked. They happen to complement each other in one dish.

Back in the day, cod was an obvious choice for a white fish recipe. Nowadays there is a huge focus on sustainability - when possible, opt for an eco-friendly choice of fish such as Icelandic cod, North Sea coley or Alaskan pollock.

Hands on time: 40 minutes   **Makes:** 12 fishcakes

Ingredients:

500g skinless white fish fillet, poached and flaked

400ml milk

70g ready to eat prawns, chopped

3 (70-80g) dill pickled cucumbers (or gherkins), finely chopped

1 medium cooked beetroot (150g), coarsely grated or chopped into small pieces

500g cooked potatoes, roughly mashed

2 tbsp dill and parsley, finely chopped

2 sprigs spring onion, finely chopped

1 tsp paprika

Salt and pepper

Breadcrumbs plus for dusting

1 egg for binding

To serve:

142g pot sour cream

1 tbsp hot chili spice blend (see my comment on page 58)

200g mixed salad

Cook cod fillet in hot boiling milk for about 5-7 minutes. Lift the fish out with a slotted spoon onto a plate. Flake it. Meanwhile cook the potatoes in salted water until tender. Drain well. Return the pan with potatoes to the hob on a low setting. Quickly mash potatoes with a fork – they should be dry and fluffy. Stir all the ingredients into the mash – prawns, beetroot, cucumbers, spring onions, herbs and seasoning. Gently add flaked cod. Don't mix it for too long otherwise the fish will break up. Add an egg to bind the fish mixture. Use your hands rather than a spoon for mixing. Form 12 patty-shaped cakes. Press into the breadcrumbs all over. Heat the oil in a frying pan. Fry fish cakes for about 4-5 minutes each side or until golden and heated through. Serve the fish cakes with a simple green salad and chili flavoured sour cream - mix one pot of sour cream (142g) with a tablespoon of hot chili spice blend.

VEGETARIAN OLIVIER SALAD

The king of salads on the Russian table is Olivier Salad, which everywhere else is known as Russian Salad. We used to scan the Zakuski spread (I explain this on page 102) on the table to make sure that Olivier has its presence. In my mind it has a distinctly retro feel. Going through various recipes for Russian Salad in different cookbooks I found out that they differ substantially. Here is my vegetarian version of the favourite salad.

Hands on time: 40 minutes   **Serves:** 10 people

Ingredients:

450g salad potatoes, (cooked in their skins); peeled and diced

2 medium carrots, (cooked unpeeled); peeled and diced

3 rounded tbsp canned peas

2 large hardboiled eggs

2 medium dill pickled cucumbers, diced

2 tbsp spring onions or chives, finely chopped

1 tbsp chopped parsley, finely chopped

2-3 heaped tbsp of Mayonnaise for dressing

Salt and pepper

Cook unpeeled vegetables until tender - don't over-cook them though; otherwise they will go mushy in the salad and then peel and cube them. Prepare all the ingredients as indicated above. Put everything into a large bowl and add peas last. Dress with mayonnaise and mix well. Season salad well with salt and pepper.

The size of the vegetable cubes could vary – some like them quite small, some, quite chunky. Due to this fact the taste will differ slightly and I'm afraid it has to be mayonnaise for the dressing. Russians also love decorating salads. For decorating they usually use the ingredients of the salad or a sprig of parsley or any other herb in use. Olivier is traditionally decorated with quarters of hardboiled egg and sprigs of parsley.

For the meat lovers you can add cooked beef or chicken - for this recipe you will need about 150g of cooked beef or one cooked chicken breast. Dill pickled cucumbers can be found in Polish or Russian shops (see stockist list on page 124).

VIRTUOUS BEETROOT CRISPS
SVEKOLNIJE CHIPSI

These little healthy babies are wonderful on their own or sprinkled on an uncomplicated green salad for brightness. If you roast them they will be even more virtuous!

Hands on time: 15 minutes

Ingredients:

4 small beetroots, uncooked
Vegetable oil, for deep frying
Salt and pepper for seasoning

Slice beetroot into thin rounds using a vegetable peeler. Spread the slices out over a platter lined with some kitchen paper; pat dry with some more kitchen paper.

Heat the oil in a deep saucepan for deep frying. Check the oil is hot enough by adding a slice of beetroot – if it's ready it will rise to the surface covered with bubbles.

Carefully put the slices of beetroot into the oil and deep fry in small batches for about 1-1½ minutes until they just start changing color and start to curl. Take them out with a slotted spoon and place on a plate covered with a paper towel. Season with salt and pepper.

To roast beetroot crisps, heat the oven to 200°C / gas mark 6. Thinly slice the beetroot to the thickness of a 10p coin. Drizzle with olive oil and season with salt and pepper. Lie flat on a non-stick baking sheet and roast for 10 minutes.

EGG AND CHEESE BITES

JAICHNO-SIRNAJA ZAMASKA

These little rye bread bites are simply irresistible. You could easily eat 4 or 5 of them without even noticing! I used to top them with Russian-type cranberries. Russian cranberries differ from the ones you can get elsewhere. They are much smaller in size and sharper in taste. Instead of cranberries you can top them with a little cranberry sauce.

Hands on time: 15 minutes   **Serves:** 8 people as canapés

Ingredients:

1 hardboiled egg, finely grated

40g cheddar cheese, finely grated

Half a small garlic clove, crushed

1 rounded tsp finely chopped parsley

2 tsp mayonnaise to bind the mixture

8 bite-size pieces of Russian rye bread, quartered and toasted

Salt and pepper to taste

A couple of sprigs of parsley for decoration

Mix the first five ingredients together in a bowl until well combined. Toast the bread and lay it on a platter. Put a teaspoon of the mixture on each piece. Decorate each piece with a parsley leaf. You can put a dot of cranberry sauce on top.

You can find Russian Borodinsky or Rossiysky bread at Waitrose and some Sainsbury's stores or alternatively, you can replace it with the German bread range "Kelderman" also from Sainsbury's. You can use a round biscuit cutter to cut out small circles. It would look fancier if you are serving these bites with pre dinner drinks. Double the quantity for a big party.

Pancakes are also a staple food in Russia. They vary in size and preparation methods. We used to make a huge stack on weekends and eat them with a variety of condiments, such as sour cream, sugar, jams and melted butter. My recipe makes 7-8 thin pancakes.

Ingredients:

150g flour,
300ml milk
1 large egg, lightly beaten
1 tbsp vegetable oil
Pinch of salt
Pinch of caster sugar

Method:

In a mixing bowl, sift the flour. Add a pinch of salt, a pinch of sugar, beaten egg and half the milk. Start stirring the flour gradually keeping the mixture free of lumps. Continue adding milk until you reach the consistency of a double cream. At the end add 1 tablespoon of vegetable oil. Make pancakes on a 25cm size frying pan.

WHITE SAUCE

It seems more complicated to make than in fact it is. You can vary the sauce by adding different spices, cheese or fresh herbs. It should take you around 15 minutes to make around 300ml.

Ingredients:

15g flour
15g butter
300ml milk

Method:

Melt the butter in a saucepan then stir in the flour and cook gently for about 1 minute, stirring constantly.

Remove the pan from the heat and gradually stir in the milk, avoiding lumps. Return to the heat and bring to the boil slowly. Continue cooking, stirring all the time, until the sauce thickens.

COURGETTE AND WALNUT DROP SCONES

KABACHKOVIJE OLADUSHKI

These are so yummy and irresistible. Put a plateful of these drop scones in the middle of the table for everyone to dig in for a Sunday breakfast or brunch. Put out lots of condiments to suit everybody's taste - jams, honey, lemon, sugar and even cranberry sauce – it is my preferred favourite. I sometimes see surprise on people's faces when they see me reaching for cranberry sauce as an alternative to jam. In the UK, cranberry sauce is only seen as a condiment for savory dishes. You can also serve the scones with salmon. Even hummus goes really well with them.

Hands on time: 15 minutes   **Makes:** 12 puff pancakes

Ingredients:

1 medium courgette, finely grated (about 150g)

1 large egg, beaten

60g self raising flour

1 tsp caster sugar

A pinch of salt

2 tsp finely chopped walnuts (optional)

Oil for frying

In a bowl, combine the grated courgette, egg, sugar, salt and chopped walnuts (if using). Mix in the flour. The batter should be quite thick. Heat the oil in a non-stick frying pan. Using a table spoon drop the batter on to a pan forming puff pancakes of about 6cm in diameter – although size doesn't really matter – just however they come! Don't let the pan get too hot – so control the heat well – you want the centre to be cooked through. If you don't want to use the drop scones straight away, pile them up into a heat proof dish, cover with foil and keep the dish in a 140°C oven.

CABBAGE GRATIN WITH SIBERIAN PINE NUTS

ZAPEKANKA IZ KAPUSTI S KEDROVIMI ORESHKAMI

Cabbage is yet another traditional Russian vegetable which is unfairly under-rated. I perked this cabbage dish up with tomatoes for some colour and pine nuts for some texture. Pine nuts, as I recall them back in my day, were slightly smaller than the ones you can get in the UK. Their origin was vast pine tree forests in Siberia. Pine nuts were usually sold unshelled so it was hard work shelling them! A collective task – again!

Hands on time: 20 minutes   **Serves:** 6 as a side dish / 4 as a vegetarian meal

Ingredients:

1 green pointed cabbage or sweetheart cabbage, trimmed and cut into thin wedges

1 onion, halved and sliced

3 garlic cloves, thinly slices

12 cherry tomatoes, halved

200g white sauce (see recipe on page 50)

30g Cheddar type cheese, grated

50g roasted pine nuts

1 tsp paprika

Salt and pepper to taste

Cook the cabbage in a pan of boiling water for about 5-7 minutes until just tender.

Drain. Transfer the cabbage into a heatproof dish. Sauté onion and garlic until tender, add halved tomatoes and cook them for about 2 minutes. Scatter on the top of the cabbage.

Pour the white sauce, sprinkle grated cheese and put dish under pre-heated grill on a medium setting for about 5 minutes.

Before serving, scatter roasted pine nuts over the prepared dish.

COLOURFUL MEAT AND SWEET PEPPER STRUDEL

MJASNOY STRUDEL S SIROM N SLADKIM PERTSEM

This is the ultimate midweek dish, relatively easy and yet satisfying. A variation of a meat loaf but a little bit more fancy.

Hands on time: 90 minutes   **Serves:** 6 people

Ingredients for the meat mixture:

500g beef mince
2 garlic cloves, crushed
2 tbsp fresh mixed herbs – parsley and dill, chopped
5 tbsp cold water
2 tbsp vegetable oil
1 tbsp mayonnaise
Salt, pepper and paprika to your taste

Ingredients for the vegetable layer:

2 mixed sweet peppers, sliced
2 medium onions, sliced
2 tbsp vegetable oil for frying
Salt and pepper

You also need:

1 sheet puff pastry (about 30 x 40cm)
9 slices of Cheddar, Edam or Gouda

Prepare the mince by adding crushed garlic, herbs, water and oil. Season. Mix well and put aside. You can prepare it the night before and keep it in the fridge.

Heat 2 tablespoons of oil and stir fry onions and sweet peppers for about 5-7 minutes. Season to taste then put aside to cool down. Pre-heat oven to 190°C / gas mark 4.

Roll the pastry out to approximately 30 x 40cm. Put cheese slices on pastry leaving 2cm around the edges. Spread the mince evenly on top of cheese. Cover mince with an even layer of vegetables. Roll up like a Swiss roll from the wide side and tuck in the ends. Put the strudel seam side down on a greased baking tray. I usually cover the tray with baking paper, grease it and dust lightly with flour. You can cut out leaf shapes out of the left over pastry to decorate the top of the strudel. Make a couple of small holes on the top of the pastry to let the air out while baking. Glaze it with egg-wash or milk and put the strudel into the oven for about 50-55 minutes or until the pastry is golden and the meat is cooked through. Serve hot with a side salad.

FISH WITH TANGY VEGETABLE MEDLEY TOPPING

RIBA POD MARINADOM

The sharpness of the vegetable medley livens up the clean flavours of the white fish. I also remember this dish being served on Soviet office canteen menus as a starter and it tasted surprisingly good! Or maybe it just seemed like it!

Hands on time: 30 minutes **Serves:** 6 people

Ingredients for the vegetable medley:

3 medium carrots, coarsely grated

1 medium parsnip, coarsely grated

1 large onion, sliced

100ml tomato puree

2 bay leaves

¼ tsp ground cloves

½ tsp ground cinnamon

½ tsp hot paprika

200ml vegetable stock

60ml wine or apple vinegar

1 tbsp brown sugar

2 tbsp vegetable oil for sautéing

1 tbsp butter

Salt and pepper

Ingredients for the meat mixture:

600g boneless and skinless white fish fillets from sustainable stock, cut into 6 pieces

3 tbsp flour

2 tsp smoked paprika

Salt and pepper

Vegetable oil for shallow frying

A knob of butter

Season fish fillets with salt and pepper. Mix the flour with the paprika on a big plate and coat the fish in the mix. Heat the oil and butter in a shallow frying pan and fry the fish for about 3-4 minutes on each side until lightly golden and cooked through. Transfer the fish carefully onto a flat dish to cool. Sauté the carrots, parsnips and onion gently in the pre-heated oil for about 6-8 minutes. Add the tomato puree, ground cloves, ground cinnamon, hot paprika and bay leaves. Mix well and add half of the vegetable stock. Let it simmer for another 6-8 minutes. Add vinegar, sugar and season with salt and pepper and the rest of the vegetable stock. Heat the mixture through for about 3 minutes with the lid on. Remove from the heat. Take out bay leaves. To serve as an appetiser, top the prepared fish with the vegetable medley while still warm. Cool down and serve cold. Sprinkle with fresh chopped parsley.

As a main course serve the dish hot with mashed potato.

HUNTER'S MEAT CUTLETS
OKHOTNICHJI ZRAZI

Why "Hunter's Meat Cutlets"? Originally, I would have thought, game was used in this recipe and whatever nature provided. There is certain produce that you associate with hunting and game and mushrooms are just two of them as they are at hand for cooking from the wild. Why not serve with my Spiced Up Buckwheat on page 58.

Hands on time: 45 minutes   **Serves:** 6 people

Ingredients for the mince:

500g lean beef mince
1 small onion, finely chopped
2 small garlic cloves, crushed
3 tsp paprika
3 tbsp oil
3 tbsp of cold water
1 tbsp of crème fraîche or sour cream
2 heaped tbsp of fresh herbs of your choice (parsley, coriander, dill) finely chopped
Salt and pepper

Ingredients for the filling:

140g mushrooms, finely chopped
1 small onion, finely chopped
1 small garlic clove, finely chopped
1 tsp paprika
1 heaped tbsp breadcrumbs
1 heaped tbsp tomato puree
1 heaped tbsp fresh herbs of your choice, chopped
1 heaped tbsp plain flour
2 tbsp oil
600ml beef gravy

Prepare the mince by adding finely chopped onion, 2 crushed garlic cloves and 3 teaspoons of paprika. Generously season the meat with freshly ground black pepper and salt. Add cold water, oil and crème fraîche. Mix it well. (I add crème fraîche, sour cream or even mayonnaise to the mince to make it juicier). Set aside.

Dry fry the mushrooms and sweat them for about 5 minutes, then add some oil and reduce the heat to medium. Add the onion and crushed garlic and fry for a further 5 minutes. Remove the pan from the heat. Mix in paprika, tomato purée, breadcrumbs and chopped mixed fresh herbs. Season it well with black pepper and salt.

Divide the mince into 6 patties. Flatten each one and put about 1 tablespoon of mushroom mixture into the centre. Fold the patty shut and shape into an egg shape. Roll the patties in flour. Heat the oil in a frying pan on a high heat. Quickly brown them all over. Transfer into a prepared roasting dish with a lid. Pour the prepared gravy over the meat patties. Make sure you have enough gravy to cover them. Put the pan into a pre-heated oven (180°C / gas mark 4) for about 35-40 minutes.

SPICED UP BUCKWHEAT WITH TOMATOES AND BASIL

GRECHNEVAJA KASHA S POMIDORAMI I BASILIKOM

I am well aware that buckwheat still needs a little more persuasion for British people to like it. And I am on a never-ending quest to find new ways to present it. When I was a child I was convinced that by eating buckwheat I would grow up to be healthy and wise. Indeed, it is a fact that buckwheat is a healthier alternative to couscous and white rice (especially quick-cook varieties). This dish is bursting with earthy goodness and might do the trick to convert some of you to like buckwheat a little more.

Hands on time: 10 minutes + cooking buckwheat   **Serves:** 4 people

Ingredients:

200g uncooked buckwheat grains
12 cherry tomatoes, halved
40g butter
½ tsp hot chili spice blend paste
15g basil leaves, torn up

Cook the buckwheat according to the recipe you will find on page 27. Melt half the butter in a deep frying pan. Stir in the chili paste. Add the tomatoes and stir fry them for about 3 minutes. Put in the buckwheat and cook for about 3-4 minutes to heat it through. Serve hot.

I use "Gourmet Garden" Hot Chili Spice Blend which I always have handy in my fridge - it has quite a long fridge life - you don't always have fresh chili peppers.

There are two rules for making short crust pastry - the proportion of flour to fat is 2:1 and the butter should be cool. The quantity I give here is for making two 20-25cm pastry cases or for one Borscht-Inspired Beetroot Pie from page 60 (with a little bit left over).

Ingredients:

250g plain flour

250g butter, chilled and diced

A pinch of salt

3-5 tbsp of chilled water (or for the beetroot pie recipe, use 2-3 tbsp of chilled beetroot juice)

Method:

Place the flour and a pinch of salt into a large bowl and add the chilled diced butter to it. Rub the butter into the flour with your fingertips until the mixture resembles fine breadcrumbs, working as quickly as possible to prevent the dough becoming warm. Add the water to the mixture and using a cold knife, stir until the dough binds together; add more cold water a teaspoon at a time if the mixture is too dry. Put the pastry on a plate, cover with cling film and chill for a minimum of 15 minutes.

BORSCHT INSPIRED BEETROOT PIE

NAVEJANIY BORSHEM SVEKOLNIY PIROG

There is a little story about the birth of this pie. When my Mum used to make Borscht she first sautéed the beetroot with the vegetables in a frying pan. The smell was so gorgeous that I couldn't resist pinching a spoonful of this flavoursome combo. When writing this book I came up with an idea to use this delicious medley in more than one way. That is how the beetroot pie was born. The filling can also be served as a versatile side dish.

Hands on time: 75 minutes   **Serves:** 8 people

Ingredients:

500g short crust pastry (recipe on page 59 or use ready-made)

2 medium raw beetroots (about 250g), coarsely grated

2 medium raw carrots, coarsely grated

1 small onion, finely chopped

3 tbsp tomato ketchup

2 tbsp tomato sauce (recipe on page 79)

1 tsp paprika

3 heaped tbsp fresh chopped coriander or parsley

2 tbsp vegetable oil

Salt and pepper to taste

142ml carton sour cream

200g mixed salad

First sauté the beetroot and carrots in vegetable oil for about 5 minutes over a gentle heat, then add the finely chopped onion and continue cooking for another 5-7 minutes. Add the ketchup and tomato sauce. Mix in herbs. Cook for another 7-10 minutes over a low heat stirring occasionally. Cool and set aside.

Pre-heat oven to 200°C / gas mark 6. Butter and flour a fluted rectangular flan tin (33.5cm x 10.5cm). Roll out two-thirds of the pastry and line the tin. Trim the edges. Prick the pastry with a fork. Line it with a piece of cut-to-size baking parchment and weigh it down with baking beans. Bake blind for 15 minutes. Remove the baking beans and baking parchment and return to the oven for another 5 minutes. Fill the case with the beetroot mixture. Beat the egg in a little bowl. Brush the edges with egg wash. Roll out a lid from the remaining pastry and lay on top of the pie. Press and slightly pinch the edges carefully. Trim again. Bake the pie for about 30-35 minutes or until golden. Cool in the baking tin and serve on a bed of green salad with a dollop of sour cream on top.

Baking blind means baking the pastry without its filling. This stops the pastry becoming soggy.

FRUGAL RUSSIAN TRUFFLES

KARTOSHKA

"Kartoshka" means "potato" in Russian. I don't exactly know how we came around to have this name for a dessert - a logical explanation would be that it sprouted from the shape.

No baking is required! They are great sweet bites for a buffet party. You can make them any size you want, depending on the occasion.

Hands on time: 20 minutes + 15 minutes chilling   **Makes:** 16-22 truffles

Ingredients:

100g butter, softened
50g icing sugar
40g dark chocolate, melted
1½ tbsp cocoa powder
1½ tbsp brandy
95g very fine breadcrumbs
1 tsp good quality vanilla extract

Mix softened butter with icing sugar until smooth. Stir in cocoa and melted chocolate (you can melt chocolate in a microwave for 3 minutes on the maximum setting) and continue mixing. Add brandy, vanilla extract and breadcrumbs and mix well. Cover the bowl with cling film and refrigerate for 15 minutes – it makes it easier to handle the mixture. Put 2 tablespoons of cocoa powder on a plate. Take a teaspoon of the mixture and form the shape of a small new potato (15g each). Roll it in cocoa powder and continue until the mixture is finished. Arrange the "potatoes" on a plate and keep them refrigerated for at least an hour or until you need them.

To get the finest breadcrumbs whizz them again in a food processor. I always make my own bread crumbs. Cut up stale white bread into crouton size pieces and scatter them on an oven tray. Pre-heat the oven to 110°C / gas mark ¼ and dry them in the oven for about 30 minutes. Cool down and store in a tin until you need them or you can blend them in the food processor straight away.

TEATIME LEMON SQUARES
LIMONNIJE KVADRATIKI K CHAJU

Lemons were one of the few items available all year around in Russia. Hence they were used in quite a lot of desserts. Tea drinking was a different affair altogether. Russians, to this day, prefer tea with lemon rather than milk. You can always tell a Russian by their tea drinking habit!

Hands on time: 75 minutes   **Makes:** 8 squares

Ingredients for the base:

80g butter, softened but not melted
100g plain flour
20g finely ground almonds
40g caster sugar
1 tbsp vanilla sugar

Ingredients for the topping:

100g caster sugar
2 tbsp plain flour
2 eggs
1 tsp lemon zest
Juice of 1 lemon

Pre-heat the oven to 180°C / gas mark 4. Lightly oil and line the base of a baking tin (approximately 20cm x 15cm size) with baking paper.

In a large bowl mix softened butter with flour, ground almonds, sugar and vanilla sugar or vanilla essence. Form the mixture into a ball, cover it and put in the fridge for 10-15 minutes.

Roll the mixture evenly to line the base of the tin. Bake for about 20-25 minutes or until it's slightly brown on top. Remove from the oven and cool slightly.

Lower the oven temperature down to 150°C.

For the filling mix together the sugar and flour in a bowl. Add eggs, lemon zest and lemon juice and blend it all with a hand mixer. Pour the mixture over the cooled base and put it back into the oven for about 25-30 minutes or until the top is firm to the touch. Cool in the tin. Cut it into 8 slices. Carefully remove lemon slices from the tin and arrange them on a serving plate. Dust slices with caster sugar.

PUSHKIN ORANGE CUP DESSERT

DESERT V APELSINOVOM STAKANCHIKE ALA PUSHKIN

There is a little gem of a restaurant in Moscow called Pushkin. A wonderful reflection of how people dined in pre-revolutionary Russia with a brilliant blend of Russian and French culinary traditions. This place entered the restaurant scene about 12 years ago and was an immediate success. Several years ago I tried a dessert in an Orange Cup in the Pushkin restaurant and was smitten by it. Obviously I never got hold of the signature restaurant recipe. I recreated it myself and made a humble copy. Now it's for you to judge!

Hands on time: 30 minutes   **Serves:** 6 people

Ingredients:

6 medium oranges
½ x 135g pack orange jelly
227g tin fruit cocktail
40g slightly roasted pine nuts
210g tin Dulce de Leche caramel sauce
½ x 142g pot whipping cream
6 fresh mint leaves

Prepare oranges by slicing the tops off and carefully scooping out the flesh. Reserve the tops. Prepare jelly following instructions on the pack. Chop pieces of fruit from the tin into even smaller pieces. Put a teaspoon of tinned fruit into the bottom of the hollowed-out oranges and fill three quarters of the orange with the jelly. Put them in the fridge to set. You can prepare the oranges up to this stage in advance and keep them in the fridge overnight. Mix the roasted pine nuts with the caramel sauce. Before serving fill the orange cups with the nut mixture. Whip the cream. Put a tablespoon of whipped cream on top. To prevent the orange from wobbling on the plate, place it on the reserved orange tops. Sprinkle with some cocoa powder and decorate with a mint leaf.

The most time-consuming task in this recipe is scooping the oranges. If you are short of time prepare them in advance. It will make your life easier on the day. You can replace tinned fruit by the same quantity of fresh fruit. If you want to show off the layers you could serve them in a clear glass.

CHOCOLATE PRUNE CAKE

SHOCOLADNIY TORT S CHERNOSLIVOM

This is a classic chocolate cake that everybody will love. A little twist to it is prunes which marry up really well with chocolate.

Hands on time: 45 minutes   **Serves:** 8 people

Ingredients for the cake:

175g unsalted butter, softened
145g self-raising flour
175g golden caster sugar
3 tbsp cocoa powder
3 large eggs
1 tsp baking powder
80g ready-to-eat pitted prunes, chopped
5 tbsp milk

Ingredients for the cream:

160g softened butter
240g condensed milk
3 tbsp cocoa powder

Pre-heat the oven to 180°C / gas mark 4.

Grease and line the bases of 2 x 18cm sandwich tins. Measure 145g of flour in a large mixing bowl and add 3 tablespoons of cocoa powder. Put the rest of the cake ingredients into the bowl apart from the chopped prunes and milk and mix well with an electric whisk. Add prunes and give the mixture another quick whisk to incorporate the prunes. You need a creamy consistency but don't overbeat the mixture. It should easily fall from the spoon. If it's too stiff add some milk.

Divide the cake mixture between two tins and bake both on the same shelf for 20-25 minutes or until the cake springs back when slightly pressed.

Cool for 5 minutes and then turn onto a wire rack to cool completely.

To prepare the cream, beat the softened butter and condensed milk together with cocoa powder.

Use the cream to sandwich the cakes together and leave some of the cream to spread over the top. You can decorate the cake with either halved prunes or sprinkle with chocolate curls.

O3
HOLIDAYS
SUMMER UNDER THE VINE

I was fortunate to spend every summer holiday with my father's family in the Northern Caucasus – a land continually exposed to the sun and therefore generously rewarding with the fruits of the Earth.

Rich flavours of freshly cut aromatic herbs, juicy ripe apricots falling into your hands and young green walnuts, transformed into delicious preserves in the skilful hands of my grandmother. Childhood memories never leave you. I used to wake up in the morning to the hustle of Grandma in the kitchen who, having already been to the market, was grinding walnuts for some exquisite Caucasian dessert or whipping eggs for a breakfast feast.

To get to that paradise in Russia, the best way to travel was by train. My vacation started the minute I boarded the train. Such trips could be enjoyable experiences in Russia in those days if you had the right attitude. It was the perfect time to catch up on reading, socialise with your family or friends, admire the landscape and, of course, eat. We had a good 28 hours to kill and we could happily munch our way through the whole journey.

You needed a food supply for at least four meals and also various snacking times. Most of the food we took with us was from home. There was a set of dishes which were a must for a train journey; roast chicken, hard boiled eggs, tomatoes, cucumbers, spring onions, a bunch of fresh herbs (we ate them raw) and some home-made cookies and sweets. We were usually served innumerable cups of tea on the train by the conductor who, as well as collecting tickets, was the guardian of the samovar.

We'd also buy bits and pieces at the stations along the way. When we reached the stations - usually quite far from Moscow - the carriages were invaded by ladies with bowls of mouth-watering foods, piping hot buttered potatoes sprinkled with fresh dill, a variety of pickles, roasted sunflower seeds in shells, buttered and salted corn on the cob and lots more. The smell was their main marketing weapon. When we eventually arrived at our destination, a welcoming supper was waiting for us. It was the first full meal in a long succession of wonderful culinary feasts.

The Northern Caucasus provided a great confluence of cuisines, Armenian, Georgian, Azerbaijani and some influence from Middle Asia.

My grandparents used to have a habit of always keeping the table laid, in case somebody dropped by. Somebody usually did. The house resounded to the clinking of cutlery and a general bustling in and out of the kitchen. Grandma was very efficient and swift in the kitchen but always light-hearted. You would never guess that she was putting any effort into cooking - smiling and singing - while filling the table with beautiful dishes and bottles of delicious homemade wine, brought up from the cellar.

Sunday in England is Roast Dinner Day but in this part of the world it is Shashlik Day! Like the Turkish shish kebab you probably know, shashlik is meat marinated with lots of onion, lemon juice and freshly ground black pepper, put on metal skewers and then cooked over wood. And, just like today, when testosterone, food and charcoal are brought together, it was exclusively a man's business to marinate the meat. Ever the alpha male, Granddad, used to say that 'the meat only likes men!' He'd marinate it the day before, with love and care. Women were allowed to help but only with vegetables and other accompaniments.

The shashlik was usually eaten with lots of fresh vegetables such as cucumbers, tomatoes, sweet peppers and big, sliced radishes with heaps of fresh herbs - coriander, oregano, parsley, tarragon, etc. Think of a herb and it was there.

Aubergines were put on skewers together with tomatoes and onions and barbecued alongside the meat. The smell of barbecued aubergines is unbeatable. Home-made sauces for the shashlik were also a key element of the feast. Grandma was graciously allowed to make these.

If the weather permitted, we piled everyone and all the provisions into cars and motorbikes and headed towards our local mountain called Mashuk, slowly creeping up the long, curvy road that wound upwards in a spiral to the top of the mountain. We'd admire the views and chat away in anticipation of the fun day ahead of us. Back at the house, in the evenings, a table would be laid outside. There we'd all sit, unwinding under the vast expanse of a walnut tree, enjoying a lazy evening tea and snacks of lovely walnut biscuits or kada sweets.

I suppose my Caucasian experience was the starting point of my irresistible desire to cook and my appreciation of food and the slow savouring of it at the dinner table.

Being quite observant when my Grandma was cooking, I learned through watching, helping, tasting and copying. I would diligently write recipes down in my brown notebook. Flipping through the yellowed pages of my first cookery notebook, you can see my handwriting developing together with my cooking skills. Back at home, I was eager to try the recipes.

At fifteen years old, my first culinary experiment took place in our small, 5 square metre kitchen in Moscow. Inspired by my annual trip to the Caucasus, I was all set to prepare a surprise dinner for my parents - to make Caucasian deep fried meat dumplings called cheburek. It took me all morning to prepare the meat filling and mix, knead and roll out the pastry, which was stubborn and did not want to stretch. Finally the last dumpling was folded. All of a sudden, I was called out and had to leave the flat for about 10 minutes, so I left my 15 beautiful, hand-crafted chebureks on the table.

When I walked back into the kitchen, I was heartbroken – Lord, my black Royal poodle, was finishing the last cheburek, licking his flour dusted mouth and looking very sheepish. Sadly that experiment was only appreciated by my dog. Still, at least he liked them. I was on my way.

PYATIGORSK GREEN BEAN DIP

ZELJENOJE LOBIO IZ PYATIGORSK

Pyatigorsk is a town in the Caucasus I used to go to every summer. For a relaxed lunch, my Grandma was always putting this flavoursome dip out on the table to scoop up with pieces of pita-like bread called Lavash. This dish is very versatile and can be served on small pieces of toast to have with pre-dinner drinks. It also makes a delicious pasta sauce with some chunks of Feta cheese stirred through. To serve 6 as a pasta sauce, you will need to double the quantity and add more oil.

Hands on time: 20 minutes   **Serves:** 8 as a dip

Ingredients:

200g green French beans, cooked
1 small onion, finely chopped
2 medium garlic clove, crushed
3 tbsp mixed fresh herbs such as coriander, parsley, basil, finely chopped
2 tbsp walnuts, finely ground
2 tbsp walnut oil (if you don't have walnut oil – use virgin olive oil instead)
2 tbsp sundried tomato pesto
1 tsp of lemon juice
Salt and pepper

Cook green beans in salted water for about 10-12 minutes until soft. Sauté the onions and garlic until translucent but not brown. Drain the beans, cut them into smaller pieces. Place all the ingredients in a blender and whizz until blended into a rough purée. Stop half way through to give it a good stir. Add walnut oil. Season well.

Picture shows Pyatigorsk Green Bean Dip and Red Kidney Bean Dip (page 76)

RED KIDNEY BEAN DIP WITH WALNUTS AND CORIANDER

LOBIO

Another dish to add up to a colourful Caucasian spread. It is another alternative to hummus and is also perfect to go with BBQ meat. Lobio can be served with an apéritif with grilled pita bread.

Hands on time: 10 minutes   **Serves:** 8 people as a dip

Ingredients:

450g can red kidney beans, drained, reserve 2 tbsp of liquid
1 small onion, finely chopped
4 tbsp fresh coriander
2-3 tbsp Virgin Olive Oil
1 tbsp finely ground walnuts (optional)

Drain the beans but reserve 2 tablespoons of the liquid. Gently sauté the onion in a tablespoon of cooking oil. Put beans in a food processor and blend them into a paste. Pour in the reserved liquid and blitz once more. Transfer into a mixing bowl. Stir in the onion, coriander and walnuts (if using). Season with salt and pepper to your taste. If the mixture is too dense add a little more oil.

SPICY SUMMER RADISH SALAD

PIKANTNY LETNIY SALAT IZ REDISKI

During a Caucasian summer, the full bounty of local vegetables is laid out before you on the table and radishes are a bright addition nestling amongst tomatoes, cucumbers, heaps of fresh herbs and spring onions. Sharply flavoursome they are eaten whole, dipped in roasted sunflower seed oil and salt. I think radishes are slightly underestimated as a salad ingredient. Here is my cool yet fiery Caucasian-inspired salad to bring radishes back to the table.

Hands on time: 10 minutes   **Serves:** 4 people

Ingredients:

1 bunch radishes, thinly sliced
½ big cucumber, thinly sliced
2 large hard boiled eggs, halved and sliced
½ bunch dill, roughly cut
150g crème fraîche mixed with 1 tsp hot chili spice blend

Place the eggs in a small pan, cover with cold water and slowly bring them to the boil. Simmer for about 7-10 minutes or until hard-boiled. When eggs are ready, cool rapidly under cold running water. Shell, halve and slice them. Slice the radishes thinly. Using a vegetable peeler, slice cucumber at a slight angle. Chop dill and mix all the ingredients together and dress it with the spiced crème fraiche.

As I mentioned before on page 58, I use "Gourmet Garden" Hot Chili Spice Blend - it's always in my house thanks to its long fridge life.

MUCH-ADMIRED AUBERGINE CAVIAR
VSEMI LJUBIMAYA BAKLAZHANOVAJA IKRA

Widely known outside the Caucasian region and almost unanimously loved by every Russian and I'm pretty sure, once tried, it will be one of your favourites too! Cooking time in the oven may seem long but it gives the dish a lovely smoky flavour. It keeps well in the fridge. Aubergine Caviar is perfect eaten cold as a dip and can be cooked in advance.

Hands on time: 30 minutes + 75 minutes in the oven   **Serves:** 6 people

Ingredients:

2 medium aubergines, cut into chunks, (approximately 300g each)

2 sweet peppers, one red, one yellow, cut into quarters

120g sweet flavoursome tomatoes, halved

5-7 large garlic cloves, whole, peeled

1 large red onion, cut into chunks

3 tbsp tomato sauce (recipe on page 79)

3 tbsp tomato ketchup

150ml virgin olive oil

1 tbsp Pomegranate Molasses (optional) (See stockist list on page 124)

2 tsp Khmeli Suneli (spice mix on page 91)

30g fresh coriander, chopped

Pre-heat the oven to 210℃ / gas mark 6. Prepare all the vegetables as instructed above and put them all into a large roasting tin. Make sure that all the vegetables are cut into more or less equal chunks.

Add oil and molasses (if used) and mix them well to coat. Season with salt and pepper and the Khmeli Suneli. Roast for 1½ hours. Ten minutes before the end of the cooking time add fresh coriander, tomato sauce and tomato ketchup.

Whizz the cooled mixture in a blender if you are using it as a dip or the topping for canapés.

Pomegranate molasses is concentrated syrup made from pomegranate juice. It is used a lot in Caucasian cooking. Hailed as the new balsamic vinegar, its sweet-sour flavour adds real depth to dishes. I love using it!

TOMATO SAUCE

This sauce is best when you can get hold of really flavoursome tomatoes when they're in season. Otherwise a good quality alternative in a jar will be perfect to use. This should take you around 45 minutes to make 1 litre of sauce.

Ingredients:

1kg flavoursome ripe tomatoes, skinned and quartered

2 tbsp tomato puree

1 large onion, finely chopped

3 garlic cloves, crushed

½ tsp sugar

½ tsp dried oregano

50g fresh basil, finely chopped

4 tbsp olive oil

Method:

Fry the onion and garlic until soft. Stir in the prepared tomatoes and the tomato puree. Cook uncovered for about 25-30 minutes on a low heat until thick and saucy. Remove from the heat and stir in the fresh basil.

You can keep the sauce in a jar for up to 5 days in the fridge.

CHEAT'S QUICK KHACHAPURI
KHACHAPURI NA SKORUJU RUKU

I can't even start on how many different types of Khachapuri exist. They differ in size and shape and they are made from yeast dough or sour dough or puff pastry. Even a layered Adjarian Khachapuri, very much resembling Italian lasagna but made purely with cheese, is also featured on Georgian menus.

In the original recipe Georgian cheese "suluguni" is used (see stockist list on page 124). The recipe you find here is my take on a well-known Georgian Cheese Pastry.

Hands on time: 30 minutes   **Serves:** 6 people

Ingredients:

1 sheet puff pastry, 40 x 27cm in size
100g cheddar cheese, grated
200g Feta cheese, crumbled with a fork

15g chopped coriander
1 egg yolk
1 tbsp sour cream
Pepper

Pre-heat oven to 200°C / gas mark 6.

Combine prepared cheeses with coriander in a large bowl. Add egg yolk and a tablespoon of sour cream. Mix well. Season with pepper. You don't need to add salt to it as both cheeses are quite salty. Spread the pastry sheet on a floured surface. Cut the pastry into 6 equal squares. Divide the mixture among the squares. Pull opposite corners together in the middle into a little knot. Make a twirl. Put Pastries on a prepared oven tray covered with a sheet of baking paper and lightly dusted with flour. Baste Khachapuri with egg wash and put them in the pre-heated oven for 15-20 minutes or until golden. Serve immediately.

As the Khachapuri have to be served piping hot, you can prepare them in advance and keep the parcels in the fridge until you need to bake them.

GEORGIAN DEEP FRIED MEAT DUMPLING

CHEBUREKI

To make Chebureki as well as their Italian brothers ravioli or Russian pelmeni is a time-consuming process and hence it is definitely a collective affair. Gather all the family together around the table and have a fun time making these tasty dumplings. The best thing to do is to make two or three batches and freeze them.

Hands on time: 35 minutes **Makes:** 28-30 Chebureki

Ingredients for the meat filling:

250g mixed mince (100g lean lamb mince and 150g lean beef mince)

1 garlic clove, crushed

½ small onion, finely chopped

3 heaped tbsp finely chopped fresh coriander

3 tbsp vegetable oil

3 tbsp water

Salt and pepper to taste

Ingredients for the dough:

300g plain flour, sifted

1 large egg, beaten

1 tsp salt

Cold water (approximately 200ml) or whatever it takes to form a stiff but elastic dough.

To prepare the dough, put the flour on the work surface. Make a well in the centre and add a beaten egg. Using a fork, start mixing them together bringing in the flour. Add water in small portions. As it begins to form a semi-soft dough, use your hands. Work the dough hard until smooth and elastic. Form it into the shape of a sausage. Cover and leave to stand at room temperature while making the filling.

For the meat filling, mix the finely minced meats with the rest of the ingredients. Roll out the dough thinly on a floured surface and cut out 12cm-diameter circles. Divide the meat mixture between the pastry circles approximately a teaspoon (15g) for each Chebureki. Brush the edge of one half with a little water or egg wash; fold the pastry over to form a semi-circle, pressing the edges together with your fingertips or crimping with a fork. Use up all the meat. Heat the oil in a deep frying pan. Deep fry Chebureki two or three at a time depending on the size of the pan. Turn over once. You have to eat them with your hands so beware of the hot juices inside!

CHICKEN IN TOMATO AND ONION SAUCE

CHAKHOKHBILI

Once again this dish is my Georgian Grandma Sofia's forté. For the best results choose chicken pieces with the skin on and on the bone. It makes the dish full-bodied and absolutely delectable. If you are fussy and don't like fiddling with bones or you are counting calories, use skinless and boneless chicken pieces. Preparing this dish in advance gives you a two-fold benefit: it allows the flavours to mingle and also makes it an easy dinner party option. But whatever you do don't skimp on the herbs.

Hands on time: 75 minutes   **Serves:** 6-8 people

Ingredients:

1.4kg chicken pieces in total (you need a selection of thighs, legs and breasts)

3-4 tbsp flour

3 big onions, finely chopped

200g tomato paste

½ a small red chili pepper, seeds removed, sliced (optional)

200ml sweet red wine (if you use dry wine, add 1 tbsp of brown sugar)

400ml chicken stock or enough to cover the chicken

3 fresh medium flavoursome tomatoes, sliced

4 heaped tbsp chopped fresh coriander

Salt and pepper

Season the chicken pieces with salt and pepper. Toss them in flour. Heat 2 tablespoons of oil in a frying pan, add the chicken pieces in batches and brown them on both sides.

Put the chicken in a big saucepan. Add finely chopped onions with the rest of the ingredients apart from fresh tomatoes. Add enough chicken stock to cover the chicken. Mix well. Simmer on a low heat for about an hour and a quarter. Half way through arrange sliced fresh tomatoes on top. Scatter a generous handful of fresh chopped coriander and continue cooking.

Rice or pasta are ideal bases for this dish. Alternatively you can serve it as it is with pieces of fresh naan or pita bread, to mop up all the lovely juices.

WALNUTS

In my Grandparents' garden in the Caucasus there was a huge walnut tree. For evening meals we used to sit down at the table under its vast expanse and have delicious Caucasian specialities.

There is an abundance of walnuts when they are in season. Green walnuts, before the hard shell is formed, were used for quite unusual green walnut jams. Sadly my Grandma's recipe for the jam is lost but I don't think green walnuts are readily available to make it anyway.

I must say it was an unexpected challenge to even find really good quality walnuts. I'd try to avoid supermarkets' or health stores' pre-packed options. I buy them at fruit and nut stalls at stations as they sell a great variety of dried fruit and nuts. As for the pre-packed ones, I prefer "Kirkland Signature". It is an American brand but I have only been able to find them in Costco (see stockist list on page 124).

To significantly develop the flavour and texture, dry-fry walnuts before using them in any dish - it also helps to remove some of the skin. I dry fry them in a frying pan on a very low setting, tossing them frequently. It will take about 10 minutes. Leave them to cool then put them in between two kitchen towels and lightly rub to remove as much skin as possible.

CHICKEN IN WALNUT SAUCE
SATZIVI

The Caucasus is the home of walnut trees which is why walnuts are vital ingredients in Caucasian cooking. They are featured in many savoury and sweet dishes. This famous Georgian dish is based largely on these nuts.

Hands on time: 30 minutes + poaching the chicken   **Serves:** 4 people or 8 as a starter

Ingredients:

4 boneless, skinless chicken breasts, poached (see recipe on page 28)

500ml chicken stock

200g toasted walnuts, finely ground (see the tip for toasting walnuts, opposite)

1 medium onion, finely chopped

4 garlic cloves, crushed

1 tsp ground coriander

1 tsp ground cloves

1 tsp cinnamon

2 bay leaves

80ml pomegranate juice or 60ml red wine vinegar

½ tsp green peppercorns in brine (optional)

½ small green or red chili pepper

Salt and black pepper

First poach the chicken pieces. You will find the recipe for poaching chicken on page 28. Cut them in half and put them in a deep dish. Reserve the stock.

Put the finely ground walnuts, finely chopped onion, crushed garlic, chili pepper and half a teaspoon of salt into a food processor and whizz to a paste. Transfer the paste to a saucepan. Add the chicken stock to the walnut mixture and add the ground coriander. Stir well and cook for about 10 minutes stirring occasionally. Mix cinnamon, ground cloves and black pepper into the pomegranate juice or vinegar and add to the saucepan together with the peppercorns in brine (if using) and bay leaves. Simmer for further 10-12 minutes. Take out the bay leaves and pour the walnut mixture over the chicken pieces. Let it cool and serve cold.

Alternatively, I discovered recently, thanks to my husband, that this dish can be served warm. One rainy Saturday my husband came home from running and I had Satsivi for lunch with a bit of green salad. He fancied a warm dish and I reluctantly took a risk and warmed the dish up in the microwave. I was pleasantly surprised by the result. So now I can recommend this dish to be served as a warm starter or a superb lunch!

GEORGIAN ROASTED VEGETABLES LASAGNA

GRUZINSKAYA OVOSHNAYA LASAGNA

This is an interesting fusion dish - a mix of Georgian and Italian tastes. They work perfectly well together as there are a lot of Mediterranean undertones to Georgian cooking. These fragrant and tasty vegetables are great either on their own with fresh ciabata or pita bread or thrown into buckwheat or couscous. They would make a fantastic companion for sea bass or grilled chicken.

Hands on time: 90 minutes + 45 baking   **Serves:** 6-8 people

Ingredients:

3 peppers - red, yellow and orange

2 medium aubergines (approximately 300g each), trimmed and cut into 2cm chunks

2 medium courgettes (approximately 150g each), trimmed and cut into 2cm chunks

2 medium red onions, quartered

1 medium garlic bulb, peeled

10-12 cherry tomatoes, halved

120ml Extra Virgin Olive Oil

2 tbsp Balsamic Vinegar

Bunch of fresh coriander, roughly chopped or torn

Salt and Pepper

9-10 lasagna sheets

430ml white sauce (see page 50 for recipe)

400ml tomato sauce (recipe on page 79)

100g Cheddar cheese, grated

2 tbsp Parmesan cheese, grated

Pre-heat oven to 200°C / gas mark 4. Place all the prepared vegetables into a large roasting tin. Add olive oil and balsamic vinegar. Season generously with salt and pepper. Toss them all together make sure they are all well coated with the dressing. Roast for about 1½-1 ¾ hours turning the vegetables over during cooking. Mix in a jar of tomato sauce and chopped coriander and heat it through. Sprinkle the base of a 20 x 30 x 6cm of lasagna dish with oil. Put a layer of lasagna sheets. Top it with ½ the roasted vegetables and 1/3 of the white sauce. Repeat layering until all the ingredients have been used. The top layer should be the layer of lasagna sheets topped with white sauce. Sprinkle grated cheeses on top. Bake in the pre-heated oven for about 45 minutes or until golden.

You can use a ready made white sauce for lasagna from the jar if you are looking for an easier way to make this recipe.

MY GRANDDAD'S SHASHLIK
SHASHLIK MOEGO DEDA

There are a hundred and one recipes for Shashlik (which has different names all around the world and kebab is one of them). But it all boils down to one thing - meat on skewers and grilled over "mangal" which is a fancy Georgian name for a BBQ. My Granddad kept saying that only men could handle Shashlik - marinating and cooking. Women just prepared accompaniments. I am quite happy to give them this privilege and just watch. Here is my Granddad's special.

Hands on time: 40 minutes + overnight marinating   **Serves:** 6 people

Ingredients:

1.2kg meat, boneless lamb, from the leg, cut into 3-4cm pieces

3 large onions, cut into rounds

Juice of 1 lemon

200ml red wine

3 tbsp Pomegranate molasses (see stockist list on page 124)

2 heaped tbsp Khmeli Suneli (see the recipe on page 91)

Salt and black pepper

Handful of fresh coriander to serve

Put the cubed meat into a large bowl. Slice the onions and add all the above mentioned ingredients to the meat. Mix well and leave to marinate overnight in the fridge. When you are ready to grill the meat, take it out of the fridge. Have 10 skewers ready about 30cm long. You should have about 4-5 pieces on one skewer. We used to have metal skewers but wooden ones will do as well. Bear in mind that you have to soak wooden skewers in cold salty water for at least half an hour before using, otherwise they will burn.

Now we come to the most testing mission – actually cooking Shashlik. In the Caucasus there was only one way to do it – in a Mangal over high heat in an open flame coal fire. Obviously it would be a challenge to have an authentic Mangal at everybody's disposal, so a charcoal grill would be the best option. A gas BBQ would come in third place. Last but not least, Shashlik can be cooked in the oven under a pre-heated grill on medium for about 20-30 minutes turning them several times until they are ready.

Cooking in a Mangal is an art, in a way, because you have to have the temperature just right – too hot and your food will burn, too low and you will be waiting forever for your meal… If you are a keen outdoor cook, try the authentic way!

PIQUANT GEORGIAN PLUM SAUCE
TKEMALI

This condiment is one of the central sauces on the table to go with Georgian Shashlik. Again, my version is adapted to the modern day; easy to make but not sacrificing on the end results.

Hands on time: 40 minutes   **Makes:** 500ml

Ingredients:

600g red or green plums preferably sour variety

2½ tsp ground coriander

6 large garlic cloves

1½ tsp mild chili powder

1 tbsp dry red wine

2 tbsp water

1 tbsp red wine vinegar

20g fresh chopped mint

20g fresh chopped coriander

2 tsp salt

Wash and stone the plums. Put all the ingredients into a saucepan. Bring the mixture to the boil and simmer for about 30 minutes. When it is ready, cool it and blend the mixture until smooth. You can keep the sauce in a glass jar in the fridge for about a month.

If you don't feel like making Shashlik you can still use this sauce with any BBQ meat.

KHMELI SUNELI GEORGIAN SPICE MIX

Khmeli Suneli is a piquant but not sharp blend of spices, traditionally used in the Caucasus, mainly in a Georgian kitchen. It is a mix of finely powdered dry herbs such as basil, hot pepper, parsley, celery, dill, coriander, bay leaf, mint, marjoram, fenugreek and saffron. Herbs are taken in equal parts and the spice has a greenish color. In an abbreviated version it contains only basil, hot chili pepper, dill, coriander, marjoram and saffron.

I advise you to make small quantities as spice mixes don't have a very long shelf life. I tend to make it in batches of 55 grams. It doesn't take more than 10 minutes to prepare.

Ingredients:

10g dried basil
10g hot chili pepper
10g dried dill
10g dried coriander
10g dried marjoram
5g saffron

Method:

Put all the dried herbs in a big enough jar, put the lid on and shake well.

You can keep the spice mix in your cupboard for up to two months.

GEORGIAN PASTRIES WITH WALNUTS AND CARDAMOM

BADDAM BURI

These pastries always remind me of the New Year season. My Grandma – an expert in baking - used to send us a parcel from the Caucasus with festive goodies and the parcel was not complete if we didn't find Baddam Burri pastries inside. It was our little ritual on New Year's Eve to hurry to the train station to receive the anticipated tasty bundle which was handed to us by a friendly train conductor.

Hands on time: 40 minutes   **Makes:** 25 pastries

Ingredients for the dough:

100g butter
160g flour
¼ cup beer or tonic water

Ingredients for the filling:

70g ground walnuts
70g caster sugar
¼ tsp freshly ground cardamom

First make the dough. Rub the butter and flour together until it is crumbly, then pour the beer/tonic water in and mix until it comes together. Make a ball, put it on a plate, cover with cling film and put it in the fridge to chill for about an hour.

Meanwhile, make the filling. Finely grind the walnuts and mix them with sugar and cardamom. Add 1-2 tablespoons of milk just enough to bind the mixture so that it resembles a paste. Mix it well.

Pre-heat oven to 200°C / gas mark 6. Lightly flour the work surface. For easy rolling, I divide the dough into two batches. Roll out the first batch of dough thin and cut out triangles (approximately 8-10cm each side). This amount of dough should make about 25 pastries. Put slightly less than 1 teaspoon of the walnut mixture along the wide side of the triangle and roll it up like a croissant. Don't overfill them otherwise the filling will come out during baking. Put the pastries on to a baking sheet lined with a piece of baking parchment paper which is lightly greased and dusted with flour. Brush each pastry with egg wash or milk and bake in the pre-heated oven for about 15-20 minutes or until golden. To make an eggwash I use one egg yolk mixed with 1 teaspoon of milk. Transfer them on to a plate, sprinkle with icing sugar and serve. Beware – they are seriously moreish!

04
OCCASIONS
THE GUESTS ARE COMING

Russians are – and always have been – hospitable. If somebody appears at their door, no matter what time of day it is or what the purpose of the unexpected visit, he will be offered food. "No" is never taken for an answer and the guest will soon find him or herself sat at the table. We Russian hostesses have superpowers when it comes to whipping up an incredibly speedy feast.

There will be a frantic clunking, as the fridge and the cupboards are searched for tins and jars. The bread will be sliced, the glasses will be laid for drinks and while continuously talking to you, we will magically unveil a totally improvised meal in front of your eyes.

Now if guests are invited over for dinner, that really is a big event. Always conscious that there may not be enough food or drinks on the table, Russians can live off bread and potatoes for days but they will lay out the best they have for a guest. Sometimes they overdo it and end up either over-eating or living off the food they have cooked for the event, for a week. Although the high cost of food in Russia has changed things somewhat now, the habit of over-cooking when entertaining, remains.

Let's start with starters - Zakuski. Russians pay a lot of attention to this part of the meal.

To begin with, the table is laid with an assortment of salads, usually about five - various cold cuts of fish, meat and game, different sorts of pickles (usually home-made) and all crowned with pirozhki. These little pasties are made out of a yeast dough or puff pastry with a filling of your choice. The most popular varieties are made with cabbage, meat or mushrooms and, as a sweeter alternative, apple. You might think you've eaten the meal already but all this is followed by a hot appetiser of something similarly filling, like mushroom or crab gratin (we use the grand term 'julienne').

But even this is not the end. The hostess then proudly produces the main course – roasted duck, chicken or pork, accompanied by roasted or boiled potatoes sprinkled with fresh herbs. Finally, when the guests cannot even get up from the table, they are offered tea from the samovar – which cannot be drunk, of course, without an accompaniment of apple pies and chocolate sweets.

If it's a special occasion, such as a birthday, there's another custom which cannot be overlooked; toasting. With vodka, of course!

At the festive table you are not allowed to drink without toasting. The person who diligently oversees this process - called the 'tamada' - is chosen at the dinner table. Their honourable duty is to ensure that the flow of toasts runs smoothly and nobody escapes their turn to make one. Even if you are not accustomed to the routine, you rapidly catch up and after the fourth or fifth toast, you are ready to participate. Actually, by that time, you're probably ready for anything!

The best toasts are witty and to the point and there's nothing worse than when a bore drags it on and on. The quality of the toasts naturally deteriorates rapidly towards the end of the evening and you are often relieved when the last word is mumbled and you can finish your (final) drink. You have to eat something in between the toasts, otherwise after the third 'bottoms up' you run the risk of suffering from a severe 'morning after'.

Rooms in Soviet apartments needed to be very versatile, often being used as a bedroom, sitting room and dining room for a big gathering. On many occasions, the door was taken off its hinges and propped on a couple of stools to serve as a table. Sitting closely around a self-made centrepiece, friends were drawn even closer together, whilst laughing away at yet another funny toast or feeling emotional over a life story probably told over and over again.

Looking back on these scenes, I feel nostalgic pangs of loss – a loss of unity and of good, old-fashioned fun. I would not want to think that this tradition had expired. Moving westwards with my family, I regret I have not encountered the same approach to the eating ceremony. My preference is for dinners that go on into the small hours and no one seems bothered about it, when we can eat food in the way in which it is meant to be eaten - savouring it slowly and enjoying every minute of it. I have tried to replicate this tradition with my family, in England - in the main, successfully. But although it's possible to relocate a whole house with all its contents from one country to another and replicate the table and fill it up with all the delights of home cuisine, the Russian soul always stays where it was born. Oh, excuse me, I seem to be making a speech. Na Zdorovje!

SMOKED SALMON PANCAKE ROLLS

RULETIKI IZ KOPCHENOGO LOSOSJA

Salmon and pancakes is a classical combo but in this presentation look different and more modern. This is a smashing party dish or it can be served as a starter. Allow 4 slices per person on a bed of green salad. Drizzle with oil mixed with lemon juice.

Hands on time: 30 minutes   **Makes:** 28 rolls

Ingredients:

400g soft cheese
2 tbsp natural yoghurt or sour cream
300g smoked salmon, sliced
4 tbsp of chopped dill
A pinch of cayenne pepper
A squeeze of lemon
For pancakes see recipe on page 49

Mix the soft cheese with the sour cream or yoghurt in a mixing bowl. Season with a pinch of cayenne pepper and a squeeze of lemon juice. Spread a layer of soft cheese on the pancakes leaving about 1cm around the edges. Sprinkle with dill, top with one layer of sliced salmon and roll them up to form a roulade. Wrap roulades in cling film and put them in the fridge for about half an hour or until you need them. Before serving unwrap the roulades, cut off the end bits and slice them on an angle with a sharp knife into about 7 pieces. Altogether you will have about 28 pieces.

You will only need 4 pancakes for this recipe but it makes sense to use up all the batter and then freeze pancakes or use them for dessert!

VIBRANT BEETROOT AND PRUNE SALAD

SVEKOLNIY SALAT

A Russian Zakuski table is a traditional spread of appetisers, ready as soon as the guests are welcomed in. It is the most important part of the meal and can range from a single appetiser, to a table full of hot and cold dishes such as fresh vegetables, pickles, salted fish, meats, cheeses and bread - and is always served with shots of vodka! This salad is the quintessence of a Russian Zakuski table and it occupies pride of place next to Olivier Salad.

Hands on time: 10 minutes   **Serves:** 6 people

Ingredients:

2 medium cooked beetroots (in total weighing about 400g), coarsely grated
1 small garlic clove, crushed
2 tbsp coriander, chopped
15g walnuts, finely chopped or ground (optional)
8 ready-to-eat pitted prunes, finely chopped
Mayonnaise to dress

Coarsely grate beetroot into a bowl. Add the crushed garlic clove, chopped coriander, chopped prunes and walnuts (optional). Add about 2 tablespoons of mayonnaise to bind the salad and mix well.

It's best to make the salad the day before. Keep it in the fridge in a container until needed.

Put on kitchen gloves before peeling beetroot to stop your hands getting stained!

Russians do love mayonnaise for dressing. If you like to be up-to-date with new trends and have time on your hands, exercise your culinary skills and prepare your own mayonnaise. You can find the recipe for homemade mayonnaise on page 114.

CHATKA CRAB SALAD

SALAT IZ KAMCHATSKIKH KRABOV

The name "Chatka" is an abbreviated form for the Kamchatka Peninsula located in the Russian Far East. The best crab meat comes from this region. Bizarrely, in communist days, tinned Chatka crab was not as much of a delicacy as it is perceived today – it was easily available and relatively cheap. So we didn't think twice about making this salad using this famous crab meat. In more challenging times or if on a budget, crab sticks were successfully used instead. If using fresh crab meat, make this recipe in June when it's in season in the UK - it's relatively inexpensive and has fabulous flavour.

Hands on time: 20 minutes   **Serves:** 4-6 people

Ingredients:

135g crab meat

140g cooked rice

2 hardboiled eggs, cubed

3cm cucumber, finely chopped

½ medium dessert apple, finely chopped

3 tbsp sweet corn (optional)

2 heaped tbsp parsley, finely chopped

2 spring onions, chopped

1 tsp paprika

Salt and pepper to taste

3-4 tbsp mayonnaise

Flake the crab meat into a mixing bowl. Discard all the hard bits. Add all the prepared ingredients and mix well. Season with salt and pepper and dress with mayonnaise.

SALMON LAYERED SALAD - MIMOSA
SLOJENIY SALAT S LOSOSEM-MIMOSA

This salad used to be part and parcel of a Russian festive spread. The preparation of this salad is fiddlier than other salads but the final result is totally worth it. It looks pretty and tastes superb. The salad has the unusual name of "Mimosa" in reference to a plant with small, round, yellow flowers. I guess it has acquired the name because grated egg yolks are scattered on top of the salad.

Hands on time: 40 minutes   **Serves:** 10-12 people

Ingredients:

500g salad potatoes (about 5 medium potatoes), boiled, peeled and grated

400g poached salmon or 2 x 213g cans pink or red salmon, drained and flaked

50g Cheddar cheese, grated

4 large hard boiled eggs, coarsely grated

½ red onion, finely chopped

Approximately 8-10 tbsp mayonnaise (see recipe on page 114)

A flat plate approx. 23cm in diameter

Prepare all the ingredients in separate bowls before assembling the salad. Cook the potatoes in their skins, peel and grate them coarsely. Finely chop the onion. Drain and flake the salmon. If using poached salmon follow the recipe on page 106. Grate the cheese and hard boiled eggs coarsely. Start assembling the salad on a big flat plate by laying half of the potatoes first. Squeeze two tablespoons of mayonnaise on top, spreading it around. Add half the salmon and a tablespoon of mayonaise; evenly sprinkle half of the onion, half the cheese, the mayonnaise and half the grated eggs. Season each layer with salt and pepper apart from the cheese layer. Repeat all the layers once again. Finish off with a layer of grated eggs. Do not put any mayonnaise on top of the salad. Keep the salad refrigerated until needed.

A cake slice is ideal for serving the salad. To modernise the dish and to make it fit for a dinner party, I presented the salad on an individual plate in a slightly different version. The photo shows this particular version of the salad. Slice potatoes rather thin and lay them on a plate first. Loosely scatter thinly sliced red onion. Put chunks of salmon on top. Sprinkle with grated cheese and crown it all with a soft boiled egg. Dress with home-made mayonnaise.

POACHED SALMON

We used tinned salmon in the good old days for all kinds of things (including the Salmon Layered Salad - Mimosa on the previous page). If you want to be a bit more posh, try poaching salmon using the following recipe.

Ingredients:

2 x 200g salmon fillets

500ml fish stock or enough to cover the salmon pieces

2 bay leaves

Method:

Place the salmon in a deep sauté pan. Pour over enough of the fish stock to cover the fillets. Bring to the boil and simmer very gently for about 15 minutes. To test if they're ready, press the point of a knife into the thickest part of the fillet - the salmon should just begin to flake. Take the fillets out and leave to cool for around 5 minutes.

SNACKY PEAR AND CHEESE GRILLED TOASTS

SIRNIJE TOSTIKI

I used to serve these as delicious tidbits if a friend dropped in unexpectedly – bread, cheese and a pear/or an apple were always at hand. It can also make a stylish and speedy breakfast.

Hands on time: 40 minutes   **Serves:** 10 people

Ingredients:

1 medium baguette (approximately 25cm long), cut into 10 slices
1 pear, thinly sliced
5 slices of cheese (choose a type of cheese which melts easily)
Butter
A jar of cranberry sauce

Pre-heat the grill to medium. Slice the baguette diagonally into even pieces. You can get about 10 slices out of a medium size baguette. Butter them slightly. First top the bread with a piece of pear and cover it with a piece of cheese. Put under the grill for about 2 minutes or until the cheese is slightly melted. Do not let the cheese run away!

As a serving suggestion, top toasts with a half a teaspoon of cranberry sauce.

You can replace a pear with an apple. A sweet variety of an apple works best for this recipe. Feel free to replace white French baguette for a bread of your preference. Sour dough bread, rye or soda bread could make a great healthy alternative.

MUSHROOM AND BEETROOT CARPACCIO

SVEKOLNO-GRIBNOJE CARPACCIO

Beetroot and mushrooms are very Russian ingredients but the way they are presented in this recipe resembles the Italian carpaccio-style starter hence the name.

Hands on time: 20 minutes + chilling the mushrooms   **Serves:** 6 people

Ingredients:

4 large St George's or Portobello mushrooms (weighing approx. 150g)
4 medium cooked beetroot, thinly sliced
30g fresh coriander, finely chopped

For the dressing:

1 tbsp wholegrain mustard
1 tsp sugar

75ml white wine vinegar
150ml extra virgin olive oil
Salt and freshly ground black pepper
1 tbsp lemon juice

To serve:

80g rocket salad
Parmesan, shaved or grated
Salt and freshly ground black pepper

Boil and peel the beetroot. Depending on the size of the beetroot it will take about 40 minutes to cook. To save time you can buy pre-cooked beetroot (not in vinegar!). Thinly slice the beetroot using a grater or a very sharp knife. Remove the stalks from the mushrooms and discard. Slice the mushrooms very thinly. Arrange beetroot slices onto plates first then add the mushrooms.

Sprinkle with coriander. For the dressing, place all of the dressing ingredients into a food processor and blend or whisk to combine.

To serve, drizzle the dressing over the mushroom and beetroot. Sprinkle with freshly grated or shaved Parmesan and season well with salt and freshly ground black pepper. Arrange a pile of rocket salad leaves in the middle of each plate.

Place the mushroom caps into the freezer for 10-15 minutes - this will make them easier to slice very thinly. Don't forget to take them out of the freezer in time! And do remember those kitchen gloves for peeling the beetroot!

MUSHROOM JULIENNE

JULIENNE IZ GRIBOV

Yet another permanent fixture on the Russian table in the old days. It was a kind of "in-between course"- a hot appetiser - after the cold Russian starters, usually represented by 10 various cold cuts and salads and before a rather hearty main course. When I think about it now, it was absolutely unnecessary for it to be an "in-between" course because it holds its own pretty well. Squeezed in between two other courses, it loses its appeal and you can't appreciate all its tasty benefits. It makes a classy individual starter served with pieces of grilled ciabatta bread or melba toast.

Hands on time: 30-40 minutes   **Serves:** 6 people

Ingredients:

250g chestnut mushrooms or you can use 200g of chestnut mushrooms and 50g dried mixed wild mushrooms, rinsed, soaked and finely chopped
1 small onion, finely chopped
2 tbsp vegetable oil

1 tbsp butter
2 tbsp flour
300g crème fraîche
3 tbsp chopped fresh parsley
2 tsp paprika
50g grated cheese (such as Cheddar)
Salt and freshly ground pepper

Pre-heat oven to 200°C / gas mark 4. Dry fry the mushrooms for about 7 minutes until most of the liquid they release has evaporated and the mushrooms are nicely browned. Add forest mushrooms if used. Add the oil, butter and chopped onion. Sauté until the onions are just softened. Add flour and mix well to coat the mushrooms. Season with paprika, salt and pepper. Mix in crème fraîche and heat it all through for about 1-2 minutes and adjust seasonings. Grate the cheese in a separate bowl. Divide the mixture between 6 ovenproof ramekins (approximately 100ml in each ramekin) - I use metal ramekins with handles (inherited from my Mum) - and then sprinkle the top of each one with the grated cheese. Place them into the pre-heated oven and bake until bubbling and the tops are well browned for about 15 minutes. Serve immediately.

If you don't have the metal ramekins I refer to in the recipe you can simply use any ceramic ones you happen to have.

LAYERED CHICKEN AND RICE DOME
KURNIK

Kurnik (derived from the word chicken-kuritsa) used to be a traditional Wedding Day dish.

Hands on time: 70 minutes   **Serves:** 6-8 people

Ingredients for the pastry:

500g packet ready-made puff pastry

For the layers:

250g cooked chicken, cut into pieces
90g long grained rice, cooked
3 hard-boiled eggs, roughly chopped
150g mushrooms, chopped

1 small onion, chopped
5 savoury pancakes (see page 49)
9 tbsp white sauce (see page 50)
4 heaped tbsp mixed fresh herbs, finely chopped
1 tsp paprika
Salt and pepper
1 small egg for glazing

Prepare the layers: 1) Chicken layer. Chop cooked chicken and mix it with 1 tablespoon of mixed herbs and 3 tablespoons of white sauce, sprinkle with paprika, season with salt and pepper. 2) Egg layer. Roughly chop hard boiled eggs. Mix them with 1 tablespoon of fresh mixed herbs, 2 tablespoons of white sauce, sprinkle with paprika and season with salt and pepper. 3) Rice layer. Mix given quantity of cooked rice with 1 tablespoon of fresh herbs and 2 tablespoons of white sauce, add paprika and season salt and pepper. 4) Mushroom layer. Slice mushrooms and chop the onion. Dry fry the mushrooms for about 7 minutes until most of the liquid they release has evaporated and the mushrooms are nicely browned. Add oil, butter and the onion. Sauté until the onions are just softened. Season with salt and pepper, mix in fresh herbs and add 2 tablespoons of white sauce.

Forming the pie. Pre-heat oven to 200°C / gas mark 6. Line a baking tray with parchment, oil it slightly and dust with flour. Roll out one third of the pastry block. Cut out a 24cm diameter circle and place it onto the baking tray. Put one pancake on top of the circle. Then alternate all the fillings interlaying them with pancakes. I suggest the following order: chicken, egg, mushroom and rice. Cover the top layer with the last pancake. Cut out a bigger circle of pastry big enough to cover your pie. Brush the edges of the lower circle with egg wash; cover the pie with a bigger circle and press the edges with your thumb or make a fluted edge with a fork. It should look like a dome. Glaze with the rest of the egg wash. Put the Kurnik into the pre-heated oven for about 35-40 minutes or until the pie is golden.

BLOODY MARY COCKTAIL

Allegedly created in 1920 by Fernand 'Pete' Petiot at Harry's Bar in Paris, this cocktail is my take on the Bloody Mary and is the inspiration for my Bloody Mary Roast on page 112. It's a great morning-after remedy for vodka-induced hangovers!

Ingredients:

125ml tomato juice
50ml vodka
15ml Worcestershire sauce
3-4 dashes of tobasco (to taste)
10ml lemon juice
Pinch of celery salt
Celery to garnish

Method:

Stir all ingredients with ice until cold, strain into a glass and garnish with a crunchy stick of celery.

"BLOODY MARY" ROAST

ZAPECHJENOYE MYASO "KROVAVAYA MARY"

This is my invention and a pure indulgence. I love English roasts but I wanted to jazz them up a little. The Bloody Mary cocktail ingredients inspired the marinade. They work perfectly well with a good piece of meat. You will judge for yourselves but I think the result is pretty impressive. And don't forget your aperitif - this Roast is crying out for the Bloody Mary cocktail from page 111!

Hands on time: 75 minutes + overnight marinating   **Serves:** 6-8 people

Ingredients:

1.2kg of top side roasting beef joint or fillet of beef

½ small carrot cut into 2cm long matchsticks

½ celery stick cut into 2cm long matchsticks

4-5 big garlic cloves cut into four thin pieces

120ml vodka

3 tbsp tomato puree

1 tbsp Tabasco sauce

½ can chopped tomatoes

Salt and pepper

Make deep incisions with the point of a sharp knife about 2½cm apart all over the beef joint. Into each hole alternate place the garlic, carrot and celery. Generously season the meat with freshly ground pepper and salt. Put the meat into a prepared greased roasting tray. Pour vodka over and roll the meat in it. Smear with tomato paste. Sprinkle Tabasco sauce all around. Cover the tray with foil and let it rest in the fridge for at least 3 hours or overnight. Pre-heat the oven to 180°C / gas mark 4. Before putting the meat into the oven, tip the chopped tomatoes all over the joint. Cook according to the Roast Beef roasting instructions or to your preference (rare, medium rare or well done). Baste the meat with the meat juices once in a while during roasting. Take the meat out of the oven, keep warm and let it rest for 20 minutes. Serve with Georgian Roasted Vegetables or Roasted New Potatoes with Garlic.

Typical roasting instructions are 20 minutes for rare, 25 minutes for medium rare and 30 minutes for well done, for each 450g of meat at 180°C / gas mark 4. If using fillet of beef, the time of cooking should be slightly shorter.

This recipe is great served with My Mum's Roasted Garlic New Potatoes on page 115.

QUICK HOME-MADE MAYONNAISE

Some of us are afraid to take on the task of making our own mayonnaise. But it's as easy as pie, especially if you have food processor. You only need a small one as you don't want to make huge quantities. You should be able to make enough for four people in less than half an hour.

Ingredients:

4 egg yolks (preferably free-range)
2 tsp English mustard
1 tbsp white wine vinegar
570ml/1 pint vegetable oil
Sea salt and freshly ground white pepper to season

Method:

Place the egg yolks into a food processor. Add the vinegar, a pinch of salt and pepper and the mustard. Pulse a couple of times to blend. Turn the food processor on and with the motor running, add the oil in a thin, steady stream through the top of the lid. After a minute or two, the mixture will change consistency as you blend and will emulsify into a thick, rich sauce. Stop adding oil when the mayonnaise has reached the desired consistency (you may not need to use all the oil). If the mayonnaise is too thick, you can thin it with a little bit of water. Taste, adjust the flavourings by adding more vinegar or mustard if desired and season with a little more sea salt and white pepper to taste. The mayonnaise can be served at once or kept in the fridge for up to a day.

MY MUM'S ROASTED GARLIC NEW POTATOES

ZAPECHJENAYA MOLODAYA KARTOSHECHKA S CHESNOKOM

These tasty little numbers are my Mum's creation. They taste delicious and look really pretty dotted around the baking dish with cute golden tops. Ideal to go with the "Bloody Mary" roast or a communal side dish.

Hands on time: 60 minutes   **Serves:** 6 people

Ingredients:

18 new potatoes of equal size, parboiled
4-5 garlic cloves, sliced
3-4 tbsp mayonnaise
50g butter

Parboil potatoes for about 8 minutes. Drain, season with salt and pepper. Grease a roasting tin. Pre-heat the oven to 200℃ / gas mark 6. Cut off the end bit from one side of potatoes and roll them in oil. Arrange them cut side down on the roasting tin. Make a slit on the top of the potatoes so you can tuck a slice of garlic and a sliver of butter in it. Put the roasting tin in the oven for about 30 minutes. After 30 minutes take the roasting tin out of the oven, dollop mayonnaise on the top of each potato and put it back in the oven till the potatoes are golden (approximately another 20 minutes).

HONEY CAKE № 1

MEDOVIK №1

I named these Honey Cakes by numbers just for fun. In the Soviet Union brands were avoided as they were considered very "western" and factories and products were given numbers to help classify and differentiate. One of the best examples was bread. Bread factories around Moscow were numbered but we also used to distinguish the quality of bread by the price it was sold for. I still remember that high quality bread was 28 kopeks, lower quality bread was 18 kopeks and yesterday's bread was 9 kopeks! In effect, we bought by numbers. I have borrowed from this to mark the differences in these two cakes.

Hands on time: 45 minutes   **Serves:** 8 people

Ingredients for the cake:

2 tbsp runny honey (preferably flavoursome type, such as Acacia or Clover)

60g caster sugar

½ tsp bicarbonate soda

40g toasted walnuts, roughly ground or chopped

3 large eggs, lightly beaten

160g plain flour, sieved

Ingredients for the cream:

40g caster sugar

250g packet soft cream cheese

80g crème fraîche or sour cream

Pre-heat the oven to 180°C / gas mark 4 Grease and dust with flour a 18cm round cake tin. Prepare the following ingredients and have them handy: grind walnuts, lightly beat eggs in a separate bowl and weigh out and sieve the flour. In a large saucepan slowly melt honey and sugar over a low heat until the sugar is dissolved and the mixture changes color slightly – it might take about 4-5 minutes. While still keeping it on the heat tip bicarbonate soda into the saucepan. The mixture starts to fizz and rise. Remove from the heat. Very quickly and vigorously mix in chopped walnuts, beaten eggs and sieved flour. Transfer it into the prepared cake tin. Bake honey cake for about 15 minutes in the oven or until the wooden skewer comes out clean. Meanwhile prepare the cream. Mix soft cream cheese with crème fraîche or sour cream and sugar with a spoon until just incorporated. Cool till you need it. When the cake is ready, first cool it in the tin for about 10 minutes. Then take it out of the tin and cool it slightly on a wire rack. While still warm cut in half and place one side on a serving plate and spread with the cream. Cover with the other half. Put some cream on the top of the cake. You can decorate it with walnut pieces. Keep it in the fridge until you need it.

HONEY CAKE № 2

MEDOVIK №2

Honey Cake 1 is the recipe from my University friend Irina Sokolova. She is an expert in Honey Cakes! The cake is denser and has a more prominent nutty flavour more like honey tin cookies. This one, Honey Cake 2 is lighter in texture as it is flourless and I use a different cream.

Hands on time: 40 minutes **Serves:** 8-10 people

Ingredients for the pastry:

120g runny honey
3 eggs
70g fine semolina
20g vanilla sugar
50g finely ground walnuts (optional)
Pinch of cinnamon
Pinch ground cloves

Ingredients for cream:

200g softened butter (not melted)
200g tin of Dulce De Leche caramel sauce

Pre-heat the oven to 180°C / gas mark 4. Prepare a square baking tin (20cm x 20cm) by greasing it and dusting with flour.

Measure honey into a glass bowl. Warm honey up over a pan of boiling water over a medium heat for 2-3 minutes. Separate eggs. Whisk egg whites until stiff. Pour in the hot honey and continue whisking until the honey gets cool. Mix together sugar and egg yolks in a separate bowl . Add whipped egg whites to egg yolks, then fold in the semolina, nuts (if used) and spices. Transfer the mixture into a prepared baking tin. Bake for about 20 minutes or until well risen and golden on top. Meanwhile make cream. Mix together the softened butter and Dulce De Leche caramel sauce - don't overbeat it! When the cake is ready, cool it in the tin for about 15 minutes and then transfer it on to a serving plate. Slice the cake in half with a sharp knife and spread half of the cream over one half, put the other half on top. Spread the rest of the cream evenly on top and put the cake in the fridge to cool completely.

CRANBERRY AND LEMON NAPOLEON CAKE

TORT NAPOLEON S KLJUKVOY I LEMONOM

Napoleon Cake is a Russian response to Mille Feuille – that is the only reasonable explanation I could give to the name. As I remember, guests were usually quite animated if they found out that Napoleon was being served for dessert. The cranberry and lemon addition to the custard cream gives it a subtle freshness.

Hands on time: 45 minutes   **Serves:** 6-8 people

Ingredients for the cream:

Russian Custard Cream (recipe on page 119) or 425g custard
8 heaped tbsp cranberry sauce
1 tsp of lemon zest

Ingredients for the pastry layers:

500g good quality ready-made puff pastry
This quantity will make 8 x 18cm circles

Pre-heat the oven to 220°C / gas mark 7. Divide the pastry block into 8 even pieces. On a floured surface, roll out one thin piece at a time. Keep the rest of the pieces in the fridge. Place an 18cm circle from a loose bottom pastry case as measurement guide in the middle, or you can use a plate of similar measurements, and score a circle with a tip of the knife (but don't cut through). Roll out the next one while baking the previous. It is just like an in-house production conveyer. Repeat with all eight pieces. To bake the pastry circles, line the baking tray with a piece of baking paper. Put one piece on the tray and prick it with a fork. It will take about 7-8 minutes to bake one until golden. Practice shows that for the first two it takes 7-8 minutes and for the rest of them only 6-7 minutes. But I still always use the timer; otherwise you can easily burn them! When you are through with all eight of them and they are cool, trim the edges of the baked circles to make them round. Reserve the crumbs, you will need them to scatter on top. Start assembling the cake on a serving plate by interlaying each circle with custard cream mixed with cranberry sauce and lemon zest. (See "Russian Custard Cream", opposite), spread custard cream on the top of the last circle. If necessary run the pallet knife around the cake to smooth off the edges. Crumble reserved crumbs and sprinkle them on top of the cake. Chill the cake for at least one hour or until you need to serve it. Leave out the cranberry sauce and the zest and you'll have a clean vanilla taste.

RUSSIAN CUSTARD CREAM

In the shops we used to buy packets of ready-to-make mix for this cream – Zavarnoy Krem. It was an easy option but tasted really good or at least it seemed like it in those days. It resembles Crème Patisserie.

Ingredients:

4 large eggs
100g caster sugar
4 tbsp plain flour
500ml milk
3 tsp good quality vanilla essence
30g butter

For the Cranberry and Lemon Napoleon cake recipe you need to fold in 8 tbsp of cranberry sauce and 1 tsp of lemon zest.

Method:

Mix eggs with sugar in a saucepan using a whisk until light and creamy. Put the saucepan on a medium heat. Gradually mix in the flour. Start pouring milk in portions constantly stirring till the mixture thickens and starts bubbling. It will take 5-7 minutes. Remove from the heat. Mix in pieces of butter. Don't forget that stirring is essential in this recipe. Leave the cream to cool. If you don't use it straight away transfer it into a glass bowl and sprinkle a little bit of sugar on top to prevent it forming a crust or cover the surface with greaseproof paper. You can keep it in a fridge for a day.

DO SVIDANYA

THE FUTURE OF RUSSIAN DINING

Perestroika brought hope. Then, excitement at the unknown, then degrees of curiosity and confusion. Having been contained for decades within iron walls, Russia opened its doors to anybody and everything from around the world. It was a spell-binding, mind-twisting change from what we, at first, perceived as nothingness to abundance. The adjusting period in the intervening years was hard and painful.

Consumers, deprived of choice, were striving for a variety of tastes and food forms and smart entrepreneurs, driven by the (now acceptable) pursuit of money, were doing everything to satisfy their hunger. The Russian market was flooded with the most bizarre selection of food items, many of suspicious quality.

Entranced by bright packaging, we were ready to buy anything - even packets with undecipherable Chinese instructions. As the years went by, the novelty of Western food began to fade away. We slowly became educated about imported food through our own mistakes, misuse and disappointment. Fortunately, we stopped judging foods randomly by their packaging becoming more au fait with their contents.

Nowadays, alongside the budget food stores, you can find well-stocked supermarkets, displaying foods from around the world, as well as the most sophisticated delicatessens. The farmers' markets preserve their authenticity and flourish, together with other retailers.

The days when you had to walk miles to find a decent eating place are also gone and restaurant businesses have blossomed. Moscow is dotted with various types of coffee shops, cafés and restaurants with cosmopolitan cuisines and a variety of price ranges.

There are more and more Russians who are prepared to pay for fine dining and the demand for this in our home market has grown. Some of the chefs now employed in our local restaurants can teach a Frenchman how to cook foie gras to perfection. The presentation of food and the ambience of the eating places can easily compete with the best restaurants in London and New York.

There is hope that balance will be found, the rush for everything Western will die out and we will see the budding of nouvelle Russian cuisine. I hope that having browsed the recipes here, you will be able to see that such an idea isn't quite as mad as it may have once sounded. You only need two things to create a great cuisine – passion and produce.

We in Russia have both. Watch this space.

Do svidanya! X

STOCKISTS

Nowadays supermarkets are keeping up with modern trends, catering for a variety of international cuisines. Asian and Polish products feature quite broadly in a lot of supermarkets. Russian food is still not greatly represented nationwide but there are plenty of Russian shops and food suppliers scattered around the UK. If you can't find them close to you, there is always online shopping. Most of the other ingredients I refer to in this book are widely available in the majority of supermarkets, apart from buckwheat which can be found only in Russian and Polish shops.

Dried barberries posed a challenge to find. I bring them from the colourful and well-stocked markets in Moscow when I am there visiting my family. These markets are brimming with all sorts of Caucasian and Asian spices. However, if you are not planning a trip to Russia any time soon then you can replace dried barberries with dried cranberries or sour cherries which are readily available from supermarkets or health stores.

The cranberry sauce I refer to in some of my recipes you can pick up in virtually any supermarket. The brands I used most here are "Ocean Spray" or Sainsbury's Taste the Difference Cranberry Sauce.

I recently discovered a great range of bakeware called Silverwood. In the "Borscht-Inspired Beetroot Pie" recipe, I refer to a loose bottom, fluted, rectangular flan tin. I absolutely adore it and recommend looking it up.

In Waitrose and some Tesco and Sainsbury's you can find "Rossisky" and "Borodinsky" Rye Bread made in the UK by "The Village Bakery". It is somewhat similar but knowing the original one very well I must say it does have a slightly different taste.

You can buy Al-Rabih Pure Pomegranate Molasses in Sainsbury's or most Asian stores.

For buckwheat, a variety of salted and pickled cucumbers, Khmeli Suneli Georgian Spice Mix, pilaf spice, rye bread, "Suluguni" Georgian cheese:

Kalinka – Russian Shop
35 Queensway
London, W2 4QJ
Tel: 0207 243 6125
www.kalinkafood.co.uk

Kolos Supermarket
Unit 6, Abney Park Ct
230-240 Stoke Newington High St
London, N16
Tel: 0207 254 6557

Gastronom
670 Romford Road
London, E12
Tel: 0208 4783 956

New Kiosk
158 Victoria Street
Victoria Arcade
London, SW1E 5ND

Babushka (Derbyshire)
71 West Bars
Chesterfield, S40 1BA
Tel: 01246 555336

Berezka
297 Finchley Rd
London, NW3
Tel: 0207 794 0777

For tinned Chatka crab meat:
www.bakersandlarners.co.uk

Polish and online food shops for buckwheat, dill pickled cucumbers, mushroom stock cubes:

Polanka
258 King Street
London, W6 0SP
Tel: 0208 741 8268

Korona
30 Streatham High Road
London, SW16

Polish Food Products
25 Rankin Close,
London, NW9 6 SR
Tel: +44 7707 233 101

www.tesco.com/polski
www.polishhypermarket.com

For Silverwood bakeware:
www.pots-and-pans.co.uk

For more information about Russian shops around the country and online shopping, go to:
www.webgastronom.com
www.russianfooddirect.com
www.russianshops.co.uk
www.garymagan.co.uk

INDEX

ACKNOWLEDGEMENTS

The concept of the book was born five years ago and has been on-and -off since then.

But all through those years, through my doubts and uncertainty there was one person who encouraged me, gave me confidence and a final decisive nudge to making this book a reality, my husband Simon.

I can't thank him enough for believing in me.

My boys, Vic and Maxim, of course, for giving me moral support and being my "guinea pigs", patiently trying my recipes over and over again. And thank you, Vic, for working on my first ever website "Russia on a Plate"– I am very proud that you are developing it for me.

My dearest Mum, Elena Gabrielova, for reliving those childhood and adolescent memories with me again and, on a more practical note, chopping, slicing, cooking and generally helping me to recreate and test the recipes. My relatives from Moscow, who in one way or the other, were contributing to this book – especially my auntie Alla. My University friend Irina, whose famous honey cake is featured in the book. My very dear friend Dianne from the Netherlands, who helped me through the toughest times in the 90s. She has and always will have a special place in my heart. My very close group of dearest school friends, who were there for me on happy and sad occasions sharing food, drink and life together (you know who you are!).

I wouldn't have done the book without a brilliant team of my creative partners – Ali Silk, Daniel Sharp and Lorenzo Piccinini from Stonewash DD&AG who fell in love with the project and made it possible for you, the readers, to see this book.

The photographer Howard Shooter who is a great person to work with. He and Emma Marsden, a home economist, made the daunting task of preparing 20 recipes for a shoot seems as easy as pie!

Thank you!

RUSSIA
ON A PLATE